The Modern Voice of an Irish Immigrant

The Modern Voice of an Irish Immigrant

by
Imelda Cummins-DeMelkon

Strategic Book Publishing and Rights Co.

Strategic Book Publishing and Rights Co.
12620 FM 1960, Suite A4-507
Houston, TX 77065
www.sbpra.com

ISBN: 978-1-61897-201-9

Library of Congress Control Number: 2011944999

Book Design by Julius Kiskis

20 19 18 17 16 15 14 13 12   1 2 3 4 5

Dedication

This book is dedicated to Cormac Gallagher......

Whose value of words encouraged me to value my own; the

spoken, the unspoken and the written.

I will forever be filled with gratitude and appreciation; his

empathy, understanding and encouragement

have been beyond generous.

His never- ending support and wisdom

are a true gift to my life.

Acknowledgments

Love and thanks to the two very special guys in my life; my beloved husband Varujan, who recognized that this was a book after reading the first few pages and who cheered me on as it continued to flow, and my son Jonathan; who inspires me every day with his own dedication to what thrills him. Thanks especially for your patience, as I spent many days and nights in my own little world, spilling the words and finding the story.

Thanks to my mother, who continues to influence my every day; the biggest compliment for me is that I am just like her. Thanks to my father, whose own love of language inspired mine; I hope my words in turn inspire him. Thanks to all my siblings, for their love and support; it was fabulous to hear so many shouts of encouragement as I made this journey.

Special thanks to John and Betty-Ann Lee, for their friendship. Their enjoyment of the first draft inspired me to keep going, and to pursue the idea of writing on a broader scale. Jennifer would be so thrilled; she remains a very central part of my life.

To my friend Ronda, our shared love of the written word inspires me and I value your input and friendship. Thanks for the many lunches around town and your unexpected notes in my mailbox.

To Marie in Urlingford, who knew? So many trips home to Ireland and your part in all of it allowed me to connect the dots. Thanks for the many, many, many years of friendship!!

To Marie in Mitchelstown, your emails brought inspiration as I fed my latest piece to the laptop, your support and friendship make life more interesting and our shared values unite us in a special way.

Thanks to Margie for the never- ending support of all three of us; your friendship makes Virginia home. I look forward to many shared cups of tea and chat.

To my Lawrence Aunt in Tuamgrainy, and my Lawrence Uncle in Cashel, thanks for the great welcome, the trips down memory lane, and especially thanks for the recipes and photos.

Appreciation goes to Fr. Tom, for his constant friendship, and the Cead Mile Failte we get every time we show up at his door.

Love to all at UCT; no visit to Ireland is complete unless I drop by.

Thanks to Helen, and remembering Richard, our lives are forever connected.

To all my other friends and extended family, I send out a big thank you, you know you are all included. Special thanks to the Editor and staff at the Virginia Gazette, for their supportive interest in all my writing, and for publishing whatever I submit.

Thank you to the readers who will read this book; know that it came from the truest place of who I am, and I hope you find hope and inspiration for yourself and your own story through my words.

Thanks to the publishing crew for your expertise and work on my behalf, and here's to the other books we will share.

In Memory of ------------------------

My beloved Grand-parents : Catherine and Thomas Lawrence of Kilconnell.

Introduction

A visit from the United States to Ireland, in the summer of 2010, primarily to see my mother, recently admitted to a nursing home and suffering episodes of memory loss and confusion, inspired me to look back at both of our lives and how the thread connecting us flows free and fragile between three generations of women. My own journey had brought me to the States in 1987, and here I was twenty-three years later, still being drawn back to my place of origin; my home. Ireland is my place of memories and traditions, of familiarity and family, the place to return to and find everything as it always was. That this might change, by the death of one or both of my parents, was something I had never given serious thought to. They had always been there, first port of call after the plane landed. I saw them getting older as the years slipped by, but my mother still cooked the bacon and sausage for our arrival day breakfast, and my father still drove into town to serve the 10.30 Mass in the Cathedral. Nothing had changed; they were still predictable and the predictability brought comfort. But reality has a way of creeping up on a person, and repeated illness and hospital stays shake up one's expectations, and force the mind to consider what is rather than what was. So here I was on yet another trip back to Ireland, anxious about

I

what I might find, and feeling more than ever the confusion of where to really call home. I knew even as I left the United States that this trip would be different to any previous visit; I would travel over the years of my existence, from my Irish childhood to my American escape. I would look closely at all the events that were somehow linked together, and finally would see the common thread. I would find answers to questions, resolution and forgiveness, and I would finally understand that home could be both sides of that ever present Atlantic divide.

Chapter One

I took a picture before I left, I am glad I did, but it wasn't necessary, because the picture of her there will stay in my head forever. Living in the United States, and hearing from my family in Ireland that my mother had been transferred to a nursing home, was one thing, but to actually see her there was quite another. I had no idea what to expect, hoped only that she would remember me and that we could have some form of conversation.

The nursing home is a converted private home, spacious with comfortable well kept gardens and outdoor space, and a large bay window that looks onto the front lawn. It is here she sits; her place, her view. This is her window to the world, as it is and as she sees it, and sometimes there's a vast difference between the two. This home has about twenty residents, relatives of someone, now passing their days someplace not their home.

The first time I pulled into the driveway I saw her, comfortably checking everything out, all who came and went, from her place in the bay window. I took a moment to watch her watch the world. I came to Ireland from the U.S. for this single moment. I would, of course, get more than that single moment, much more, but this was enough

3

then. I went close to the window and made eye contact, and her face lit up like Christmas as she shook her hand to wave me in.

The relief in the recognition was huge. I knew the details of her situation, but I had not seen her for a year, so didn't know the full extent of possible change. She has vascular dementia, and in her case it presents itself as confusion. Not all the time, and not always the same, and so it's a case of take me as you find me. And we do, and Thank God for the opportunity.

I went in and kissed her, and saw she was not so changed. Lots of questions poured out, and I was so thrilled to reply, because everything she asked made sense and I thought, "what a blessing and she is still here". That lasted for a few minutes, and then she asked me why all the other people were driving in to turn their cars in our driveway. I realized she thought she was at her home. I took a minute and told her there was some sort of traffic jam, and we had told them they could. She relaxed. She asked how the flight was, and how was my son. She told me she loved my hair, and asked if my husband (a Gemologist and Master Jeweler) had made the jewelry I was wearing.

Then she wanted to know why her husband hadn't come back, he only went to put gas in the car, so where was he? She became agitated, why isn't he back, is he coming back? The sudden panic emanating from her was hard to see, and I thought of something to distract her. I reminded her that the gas station is also a car wash, and we remembered together that that's probably what's taking so long. We can both see him washing his car and being so meticulous about it. She visibly settled, the problem solved; an acceptable explanation. Then she said I had better go, her parents were coming to take her for a drive, and "anyway", she said, "you will come see me again". I left her there, seemingly happy and content. Outside, I stood in front of her bay window and I waved and blew her a kiss. She smiled and waved, and I left, happy.

As I drove away I remembered. I remembered too much and too little. I wanted to store it all in a safe place in my brain. I wanted to remember for her, and find a way to get her to remember with me. I felt a huge sense of loss; but she is still in the window. I found comfort in knowing that I could see her, and visit with her, many times over the next ten days. Even though we have had many visits together over the years, her deteriorating health has brought the urgent sense of unfinished business to the fore. She moves between the past and the present, and I need to grab the moments in the present with both hands, and find the answers to questions that I cannot ask directly.

I travel back in time with my memories, and there she is; tall and strong and laughing and talking and listening and sharing and advising and loving and wanting and just is...there. Her parents' house and where and who she came from figure strongly in my memory trip; the solid stone farmhouse, the farm smells, the work of life evident, and the joy of family and a predictable way. It was hard because it was basic, but it was comforting because it was hers and where she came from. I was part of it because it was given to me, and it was shared; part of her. Will I keep these memories always? That question is too hard to think about, it has to be enough to still have them now.

I remember the narrow road that led off the main road to the farmhouse, the smell of cows and hens, baking bread and fresh fruits, flowers and vegetables; all mixed up together. I remember the sounds of the horses, as they set off on the daily run to the creamery, the churns rattling and the crow's chorus following, as the main road got closer. We loved it, and only now that I am older do I realize it was hers first. It is different certainly, for each of us, but definitely hers first, and now that she is confused am I remembering for her? Is she remembering this? Perhaps she is. She told a visitor one evening, as they chatted with her in her window, that she was exhausted from milking all the cows. I know from her siblings that she may have milked one or two cows, but never the herd.

The details and accuracy are irrelevant, the point to savor is that the place is where she is, and I can understand her need for the comfort that this memory brings her. I feel the same comfort as I remember childhood holidays at the farm, and my mother must sense our shared love of the life that was hers, and that I too came to love, as a part of me. She can remember safely with me, some of the words understood if left unsaid.

The next day I get the same welcome, and I settle in beside her chair as she tells me all the news. After a minute, I notice she is crying, and the sight of this is too much. How can I comfort her? She tells me there was fighting and it couldn't be stopped, so her husband had gone to get the Gardai or police. "You know I don't like the fighting and shouting", she says, "I just can't take it". I tell her it will all be sorted out, and that I agree she shouldn't have to deal with it. She is comforted by this and I can tell she is calming down. I find a tissue in my purse and help her get composed, and reassure her again, that her husband will be back soon, having taken care of it all and she agrees with "he will".

I notice she has put my purse on the tray that's permanently affixed to her chair (to prevent a fall as well as be a functioning table for her). She proceeds to take everything out and admires it all. I realize that she thinks it's hers, and she explains to me the uses of everything she takes out. I enjoy this enormously, especially when she takes out my wallet, looks at the Euro and Dollars and whispers with great conspiracy, "and I thought I had no money, and sure I have loads of it." We both giggle together. It's so personal for me and something she would never have done, always respectful of another's belongings.

Two minutes later she is telling me she loves my purse, and there's no mention of her thinking it was hers. I have to wonder if her comments are a releasing from another time. Is she remembering the arguing that I grew up with and her own experience of limited control with personal funds? I will continue to listen carefully to whatever part of her story she wants to share. I already know, unconsciously, that the big picture will wait to fully come together until I return to the States.

She tells me her brother, John, came to visit, how he is great, very good to her. She only knows he was there at some point, maybe today, yesterday, or even last week. This is very hard to hear because I wonder will she remember the time we are spending together; after I return to the States. I didn't think it mattered, but it does. I am not ready yet to be back in my own life, so I will continue the memory trail with her, and together we will make it clearer.

A nurse brings her a tea tray with small ham sandwiches, a slice of cake, and the inevitable pot of tea. I pour her a cup of tea and she picks up a spoon and liberally spoons in the sugar. I watch in fascination as she opens up the sandwich and spoons some sugar onto the ham. I wonder if she really intends to eat this sugar sandwich, and sure enough, she happily munches away, repeats the process on the next sandwich and the same reaction follows. She comes 'back' for a moment, only to say, "I know I shouldn't be eating all this sugar, but I don't care, I really don't". I agree with her, who cares as long as she is enjoying it. Later, I remember that her mother used to do this for all the younger children, to entice them to eat, as indeed she did herself for us when we were small. Perhaps another scene from the past is playing out in her head. I don't actually care either, about too much sugar, I can only enjoy the fact that she is enjoying the food, and I am also enjoying her sense of indulging herself; like a kid taking too many cookies from the cookie jar.

In the middle of all this feasting, she asks me if I can drop her home. I say, "of course, just let me do a quick errand and I will be right back". She is thrilled with herself; she waves me off and tells me to be careful, and then, "hurry back". I feel a little guilty about not being honest with her, but sometimes you know that the final goodbye can be left unsaid. I know from talking with the nurses and others that this is the best way. After I leave, she will go back to looking out her window, and she will seem to be waiting for another person to arrive, so that she can wave to them to come on in.

I arrive early one morning, and she is not quite ready to start her day. The nurse tells me to go ahead to her room, so I do. She is sitting in a chair beside her bed, cozy in her robe and she looks like she had a good night's sleep. She loves to hear how well she looks, and I love to see her so content. I don't see her as the 'Woman in the Window' in this moment, and it seems like I could almost be visiting with her in her own home. We chat about the lovely sunshine, I tell her there was a baptism down at the Cathedral; as I passed I saw a baby all dressed up being carried in. She tells me that's where her husband is; helping out.

Her mind wanders to the early years of her marriage, and perhaps to the days of her own babies being baptized, and she talks about having lots of small children, very close in age, and how she managed. She tells me she couldn't do it now, and we both laugh at the very idea. She tells me how helpful her mother was, and how often they got together. We reminisce about all the food that was cooked and baked in her mother's kitchen, and she reminds me of all the cousins that she grew up with. Once again, I am fascinated by the moments of complete clarity. I join her and remind her of homes and people we visited, and I can see the pictures lining up behind her eyes, and I hold on so carefully; I want to stay until she can say the words. It's so tenuous, but having so much respect for the fragility, I can take it slowly and be patient. The pictures are in my own eyes now, and I can share, and once she realizes that we are in the same place, she walks so steadily that I end up just trying to keep pace with her. I see her happy and full of fun and life. So sociable and enjoying every moment, surrounded by all she loves. It's a rare treat to get a glimpse of your mother before you were even born.

She takes the fabric of what I am wearing between her fingers, to appreciate the softness and talk about the texture, and it reminds her of her earlier working life, before she got married. She and her sister ran a dress-making/tailoring business. We chat about all the beautiful clothes she made. She dressed brides for their special day, and babies for their christening, first communion and confirmation, and made

suits for other occasions. She created her own wardrobe;
beautifully tailored coats and jackets and skirts and dresses.
My photographs show me her talent, and I take a moment
to give thanks for her sister's generosity in giving them to
me. I remind her of specific outfits she made for her own
children. When, for example, she dressed all of her daughters
in different colors of the same dress, and the joy that comes
over her face is so much more than the colors of the dress.

She made a christening gown from her wedding dress
that all her children wore, and was passed down to me, the
care-taker. I asked her if I could borrow it when my son was
born, sixteen years ago. She was delighted, as he would be
the first grandchild to wear it, and so it became mine. She
smiles and I know the memory has popped up for her. I
want to tell her so much, but it's a time for listening. She
shares with me that the staff here can't believe that she
has twelve children. I am excited that she remembers her
children. I want to freeze time, to try and stop the confusion
from robbing her, robbing me, but I know that I can't. I am
grateful for this oasis of opportunity; where she and I can
chat and wander around her memories.

I feel so connected to her, and so thankful that she is
aware on some level of what I need, and that she just gives
it all to me. I will make sense of it later. I instinctively know
that she is comfortable going back to when her parents, my
grandparents, were still alive. She knows I want to hear it
and that I want to take the journey with her. I am reminded
of the love and the simple life of my grandparents' farm,
and how it allows patience and a hunger for my mother's
mind to continue with the sharing.

I have already been here over a week, and I cannot believe
how few days I have left. On some level, I know that what

I am experiencing is different to my previous visits. When I am with my mother it's like being in a bubble; insulated from everything going on around us. I am in the moment of every moment with her. On my way to visit her, I stop at a convenience store close by, and pick up a magazine and an ice-cream. Again, I stop by her window, and she lights up and waves for me to hurry in. We eat our ice-cream and enjoy our magazine, and she slowly reads every word out loud. She studies the photos carefully, and comments on everything, from the fashion to the BBQ grills. She sees the girl in the magazine is wearing a sweater just like mine, and for a second she wonders if it is me in the picture. It's flattering and funny, and such pure entertainment.

She sounds so clear and so full of enjoyment. Is she aware of what is happening in her mind? I hope not. I hope that we are the only ones mourning what is lost. Today she is distracted by the other people around the place, and she tells me she wishes they would all go home. She does not remember inviting all these people. Not for the first time, I am thankful for the sensitivity of those around her. Nobody contradicts or questions her, and it makes it easier to go along with whatever she is saying. In a moment of clarity, she tells me she will miss me when I leave, and do I know my husband thinks the world of me. I could cry, and it is an effort not to fall apart and tell her how sad I feel; that she is only really here some of the time. I want my mother back. I hope she knows, on some level, the gifts she has given me on this trip home.

It's another day, almost my last, and the sun is shining in her window, and she is totally involved with rearranging the curtains. She has waved us in, my son and I, so on some level she knows we are with her. She continues to fiddle with the curtains, trying to tie them up and move the fabric out of her way. She wants a better view to the outside, too stubborn and distracted to realize that she is blocking the view instead. She abruptly picks up a book, and asks if she can read to us. She has had enough of the uncertain world she is in now, and the comfort of the familiarity of joyful reading is calling her.

This is a moment when I want to stop time, to listen to her read the words with total involvement and understanding. I want to hold onto this, because it is so much of who she is/ was? A book lover, a reader; I see her at the library stocking up, I see her curled up with a book in the living room by herself. I see her lying in bed; a break from her life with a book, and I see her on the beach, another book. I filter out all the other sounds and just listen. She seems not to be the 'Woman in the Window' anymore; she is my Mother, refreshing the strongest memories of her that I have, and I listen and I remember, and I know from her enjoyment that she is remembering too.

For both of us, it's all about the words; whether you read them, say them or just know that they're there. She has made the connection, shared it, and passed it on. I am happy to be on the receiving end, and I will allow her words to guide me as I find my way back; knowing that this will be the only way forward. This is her story, this is my story-----this is how I see it.

Chapter Two

My parents met in the early 50s, both in their early 20's. They married in 1955 and would go on to celebrate over fifty-five years as a couple. They were an unlikely couple in many ways. She was a farmer's daughter, was raised in relative comfort, and knew the value of a day's work from watching the demands of life on a farm.

She was one of nine; five sons and four daughters. Her sister tells me she was 'favored'; could do no wrong. From photographs that have come to me from various sources, I see a good looking, self-assured woman, who seems to have lived a fairly social and fun life. She had two involved parents; her father ran the farm and her mother ran the home. Her father was conservative, forbidding too much socializing beyond their immediate circle. They were not permitted to indulge in anything he did not consider necessary, for example, the vulgar vanity of nail polish! From stories, I know she was a risk taker with a strong will of her own, defying her father and sneaking off to what were called the 'platform dances'. These platforms or wood bases were set up in villages, and once the music started, everyone was out and dancing. Young people biked from the neighboring area, threw their bikes in the grass, and danced into the early hours. Her parents used to go to the movies every Sunday together. My grandfather was a fan of the westerns, and she would be ready to flee as soon as they were gone. She didn't always make it back on time, and the price she paid was an earful of how she had no sense and would come to no good.

My grandparents and their children lived the rural life of daily demands on the farm, and the hard work of everyday chores in the 30s and 40s.They had what they needed, but kept life simple. They knew their neighbors and their social life was easy; visiting their neighbors and nearby family, cups of tea, homemade bread and jam, and conversation. She, their daughter, had a dress making/tailoring business with her sister in the town of Cashel, County Tipperary. She was talented and popular and enjoyed the work.

She had older siblings, but only one brother was married before her, so she had a less strict time in her late teens and early 20s. She had older sisters and also one younger sister still at home, helping around the farm house and the farm. She had an easier time of it because of this, and got away with doing less, as the older ones were called on first. Her brothers were going to dances so she and her sister tagged along. She tells me stories of all of them riding their bikes around the country roads, and getting together at various neighbors' houses. They had the freedom of the times; the late 40s and early 50s when everybody knew everybody else, and that was still a good thing. She was, even at this early age, very interested in fashion and her own clothes. From the photos of that time she loved the classic tailored look; the fitted pencil skirts and the soft wool sweaters.

Chapter Three

My father's family life was less calm, and less clearly defined. He was one of eight; he had two brothers and five sisters. His father had a drinking problem, and life went on around the problem, and his mother ruled the roost. I remember as a child going in the car with my father, to pick his own father up off the street, literally, to deliver him back to his home. So drunk he didn't know where he was. His mother would meet us at the door, no reaction that I could see; this had all happened so often that it was an accepted routine. She would hand me a bar of Kit Kat or Cadbury's, and we would return home. My father would say this is all "terrible", and remind me not to talk about what we had just done, or anything I had seen.

His mother was a strong personality, who seemed to believe that her opinion of the world, and the people in it, was the only one worth considering. From the distance of age and time, it's clear that her method of raising children was to mold them in her own image, or perhaps raise them as she was raised, and the most important lesson she could teach them, was how to provide. She ended up creating eight people who, on the one hand, were motivated go

getters and self starters, but on the other, were seriously
crippled emotionally. They were raised to be in control,
and became adults who gave great weight to showing a
strong face to the world. Outward appearances outweighed
all else. Never ever tell anyone else your business. This is
too simplified, but they are bunched together in my mind,
because they all inflicted this unhealthy style onto the next
generation, which is mine. All of the grandchildren of my
father's mother paid the price, one way or another.

There is no excuse, but in the interest of tentative
understanding, I would say it's all they knew.

Chapter Four

My parents met in Cashel, County Tipperary, literally talking on the street; he was selling Insurance and she had the sewing work locally. They took their time getting to know each other and frequently made plans to go to a dance together. They would go in groups with her siblings and his siblings, and the extended family of cousins and neighbors. Initially, when these two came together as a couple, my mother brought a calm balance to the relationship. He was seeing in her something he had never seen before. It was a novelty to talk to someone and have your views heard, without the kind of assumptions he had grown up with.

They were engaged to be married a year after they met, she broke it off for some reason, and they came back together about a month later. They were married soon after, and decided to set up house, having found a small apartment in the town where he had grown up. Her first child was born and the pattern for her life was thus established. As her babies were born, she nurtured them. She had her own mother close by, and her connection to her own family was still strong.

I assume, in the early days, she was still in ignorant

bliss, and, cushioned by the love, had no way of knowing that their differences, especially with regard to parenting and the expectations of one's children, were far beyond anything she could comprehend. As her children got older, it would become more apparent, but for now, she still had sole care of these little people. By the end of 1960, she had five children under five, and she was twenty-nine years old.

Chapter Five

My own recollection of family life as a young child is happy. My mother's family features strongly. My connection to her parents was very close, and I identified with the home life at the farm, and enjoyed the luxury of the freedom and safety and simplicity of it all. The sounds and smells of farm life, and the lifestyle there in the 60s and 70s will stay with me always, and formed the core of who I would become. My grandmother loved her grandchildren; was generous in having us during all the holidays, and knew that we always wanted to stay longer.

The older of my mother's children spent the most time there. It was a help, I am sure, to my mother, to have somewhere safe to leave us, where she knew there was lots of built in entertainment. Her mother was a nurturer, and so she was safely exposing her children to what had been her own earlier life. As her family continued to grow; there was always a new baby and a toddler around, it gave her time to devote to her smaller children, when the older ones were at the farm.

In those early days my mother's three single brothers were still living at home. My Uncle Thomas would tend the vegetable garden and coax the berries for jam making. He was always kind to us; allowed us to help with the berries and pulling the vegetables. He would also show us what flowers he had planted, and which ones, once in bloom, could be picked. On many a trip there to pick us up, or just on a visit, my mother would return to her own home with a big bouquet. When the fruit was ready to pick, we would fill up buckets for my grandmother to make her jam, or pies. I can smell the pie cooking, and we would have to wait patiently until it was ready. Sometimes she gave us one fresh out of the oven, wrapped in a tea towel, and we could take it up the fields to eat.

My Uncle Gus was the top farmer, especially after my Grandfather's death, in 1966, when my mother was thirty-five. He was the one who made the decisions, and oversaw the day to day running of the place. He bought and sold livestock, decided what crops to grow in any given year, and was the one to keep everything going. He babied the calves and showed us how to also. He kept the farm horses in the pasture long after they were useful on the farm; knowing we enjoyed the freedom of riding the horses around the fields. He worked hard seven days a week. Many a Sunday, I remember standing by the stone wall, leaning in to the cow house, chatting with him as he milked the cows. If we wanted to do anything outside the farmhouse, he was the one to ask, and he would happily take time out of his day, to show us whatever.

One year, we whitewashed the cow house, and painted up names for all the cows. We were town kids, and this kind of freedom to slobber around with a paint brush was sheer heaven. No matter how busy he was, he would always stop and take time for us. Mid- afternoon, he might have to make a quick trip to the shop at the creamery, and off he'd go in his wellington boots and farm clothes, rolling down the window as he got in, to ask if we wanted to come too. We jumped at the chance. I was always fascinated by the array of stuff at the creamery shop. The ceiling was dotted with hooks and pulleys, and everything and anything was seen hanging there. There were pots and pans, beside rubber boots, beside a gadget for who knew what, beside sacks of flour and sugar, beside a spare tire, and maybe even a winter coat. Behind the counter were the sweets; the big glass jars of unwrapped candy, that you bought by the quarter pound, and were wrapped in whatever was handy. It was total chaos to my eyes, after the order of my father's store, but magical at the same time. I was fascinated by the idea of being able to buy so many different things, all in the same place.

My Uncle John was around sometimes, but I mostly remember that he was a builder, and off doing that during the day. He would often drop in, with a guy he worked with, just for a quick cup of tea and a hunk of homemade bread, on the way back to town.

During our holidays, when we stayed there, our days were made up of trips to the creamery, collecting the eggs, feeding the chickens, watching my grandmother make her brown bread and currant cake. We were free to enjoy all aspects of farm life, with few restrictions, except in relation to safety. We strolled down country lanes and roads, we walked to the little shop in Mockler's Hill, and we visited neighbors. We saw baby calves arrive and cows loaded to leave. We fished for tadpoles with our jam jars, and we swam in the river.

A tradition during the main meal of the day; I can still hear the radio beep for the 1 o' clock news, "this is Maurice

O'Doherty with RTE 1", my grandfather would shout "whist", and total silence would descend. We wouldn't make a sound; this was his sacred time to hear what the world was up to beyond the fences of his farm. I can still smell the onions frying, and hear the sizzle. Dinner was big slabs of beef or bacon, all from the farm, a big pot of potatoes thrown into the middle of the table, and garden veg. We helped clean up, after the men went back to farming.

Occasionally, we would hear a car coming up the lane/ driveway, and it might be a cousin or a neighbor, and there followed a couple of hours of chat, tea and whatever was baked that day. If it was one of my grandmother's days for visiting, we would head out to family or neighbors, for more of the same. None of my grandmother's children moved too far from home, so it was easy for her to visit. We would set off, my grandfather driving, to one of my aunts or uncles, and spend an afternoon of rambling around more fields. One had a big orchard, and we would climb the trees and pick the apples; sometimes eating them and other times filling huge baskets. A lot of them would be headed for sale at a local market. I remember loving the idea that after an afternoon of all this outdoor freedom, and a supper of home cooked and possibly home cured food, and homemade bread and pies, I would get to go home with my grandmother. To my child's eyes it seemed like a holiday within a holiday. Whether we were at my grandmother's, or visiting another farm, all of the children would be mostly outside, chasing each other around the fields. We would play hide and seek around the bales of hay, and generally enjoy the total freedom of this rural heaven.

One of the highlights of a visit was when my grandparents would get into their town gear, and we would head into Cashel.

My grandmother had her good coat on and solid leather shoes with a heel, and her purse hanging from her arm. My grandfather wore a suit and his fedora. In my child's eyes I see him walking tall, up the steps of the bank in Cashel. I thought he owned the town, he looked so grand and powerful. I don't mean figuratively, I mean it literally; I thought the whole of Cashel was his. He inspired this kind of thinking; so proud and confident of his work and his family.

We would go with my grandmother, for the shop bought stuff for the farmhouse, and be treated to brown bags of sweets, no charge, by the local shop keepers. They knew who we were and loved to treat us. We were the grandchildren and my grandmother proudly showed us off. Evenings, back at the farm, after supper of rashers and sausages and brown bread, we listened to the radio, or my grandmother showed us how to sew and knit clothes for our dolls. The Uncles would be getting ready for a night out. I can still hear the water splashing in the scullery, and remember the strong smell of the slab of soap. They had metal things in their hair to create waves, and my grandmother would be standing by, with a clean starched shirt. And then they were off; sometimes to play badminton, and sometimes to go to dances. They would have been in their early 20s and 30s. My Uncle Thomas would clip up his trousers and head off on his bike. He was a known figure along those country roads, and it was a time when everyone knew everyone else, and probably where they were headed. He was off to neighbors to play cards. Next morning, when we came down to the kitchen, there was a bag of mixed sweets; colleen and iced caramels, picked up just for us.

Sunday would roll around, and the morning was a ritual of frying bacon, uncles polishing shoes, tying up Saturday night washed hair in ribbons, and getting ready for Mass. Sometimes we went to Cashel and sometimes we went to Fethard. Driving into Cashel, I can still hear the engine of my grandfather's Morris minor straining; years later, I realized, he always drove in the wrong gear! Sunday afternoons, we disappeared into the fields with the horses, Bud and Jacqueline, or we played games, or just jumped hay stacks. We hoped we wouldn't hear my father's car, coming to pick us up. No car arriving meant we could stay another week. I can still feel the relief and joy, when Kilconnell, as my mother's home place was named, was ours for another week.

Some of my fondest memories are of the days spent saving the hay. For a couple of days beforehand, there would be discussions about whether it was ready; the right color or texture, and then watching the weather forecast. There would need to be an entire day of dry and preferably sunny weather. Once the day was decided on, word got out, and everyone showed up to help. My Uncle John would stay home, and his builder friend Jimbo would come to help too. My Uncle Gus was all business, and had a system in place; where everyone knew what their job would be, so that the hay would all be saved before the sun went down. We were, of course, looking forward to all the fun and activity, and to helping too.

The tractor and trailer would be pulled close. After the hay had been cut, and enough bales had been gathered, the first trailer load would be piled on with pitchforks, and then driven up the lane to the barn. There would be two teams; one gathering the cut hay and piling it into mounds, and then the second team would load the trailer and sit up on the back. Once at the barn, they would help to unload. We loved to sit on top of a mound of hay and go along for the ride.

Around midday, my sister and I would return to the farmhouse, and help my grandmother put together a meal for the crowd. There was too much to do to take a break in the middle of the day, especially while the sun was still shining, so we would carry the food to the field. My grandmother would make sandwiches; big slices of cooked beef between two hunks of homemade bread, all loaded into a basket. She filled tin cans with tea, milk already added, and she would put sugar wrapped in brown paper into the basket, and my sister and I would head back to the field. Everyone would find a spot on the ground, or on top of a mound of hay, and dig in. It was the best food ever, made more delicious by being eaten outdoors, with the sun shining down on us and the lazy pace of idle chat. No clock watching, just good food and time to enjoy each other and the quiet. When we were all done eating, the work would resume.

Sometime around 3pm, I would look to the farmhouse and see my grandmother waving a white cloth. This was the cue to come on back with the empty tin cans and she would refill them. We would head off again with the new supplies; the cans of fresh tea, and this time the basket would have slices of fruit bread held together with jam, and slices of apple cake. We were always reminded to walk carefully, so as not to spill the tea. It was a time of simple food and simple pleasures.

After all the hay had been brought into the barn, we would head into the farmhouse, for the 'big' meal. My grandmother and a few neighbor women would have prepared a feast. Everyone stayed to eat, chat and enjoy the postmortem of the day. How the hay was, compared to last year, and how much help we had been. They would all wander off home, some only walking distance away. And so

ended a day of hay making and we were always sad when
the day was over; it was the only job that needed everyone
working in the same place and at the same time. It was a
child's ideal; safe and fun, and childish innocence allowed
us to believe it would go on forever.

Chapter Six

Interaction with my father's family was very different. For starters, even though they lived nearby, we actually saw very little of them. Any dealings my father had with his family, were, by and large, kept separate from his own children. There were no Sunday gatherings hosted by my father's mother, this was definitely not her style. Interesting though, that we never asked to go there, stay with her or have her over. By contrast with how it was with my mother's family. We were not embraced as grandchildren; it might explain why we always referred to her as my father's mother.

Interaction was not relaxed; there seemed a pressure to give the right answer, and not being sure what that was. I remember being quizzed, that's what it felt like, and to them it was just everyday conversation. This was the style of communication they were raised with, how his mother interacted with all of them, as they were growing up; the hint of a threat in every word. I remember seeing the other person standing, waiting for a detailed answer, or more questions would follow. It left a feeling of being accused of something, and you had no idea what, except thinking you must have done something wrong.

This was the style of communication my father used with his own children, and served as the basis for a lot of the doubt and uncertainty that would plague each of his children, as they moved through the teen years and further. I can make this observation now, backed by the luxury of my own search for understanding as an adult, but looking back at us as children, we were immersed in confusion and uncertainty. I think that as very small children, we could only have been aware that we saw two people, (our parents), talking to us in two very differing styles, and this gauged only by how you felt. I remember not having the ability to verbalize, but knowing this was a little off. For me personally, it was only as I got older, that I reached a better understanding, and realized that nothing I did could change how my father would talk to me. He must have always sensed impatience from his own mother, because he certainly had no patience with us. Give the right answer, and fast. Always in survival mode; a feeling of high alert needed for self protection. I think that while my father and his siblings might now be puzzled, by the problems/ difficulties of their adult children, and it is a giant step to even assume acknowledgement of any problems, they have no idea of the origin.

For me as an adult, I find comfort in knowing absolutely, that they had no clue of the consequences of their actions. I am not making allowances for them, or for their behavior; I am simply stating the fact. They didn't question the health of their own emotions or even lack of them, so how could they ever think of ours. They would see themselves as having done a good job, certainly by the standards of their own mother, and by the standards of the world they themselves lived in. Most, if not all, were business owners, and they all provided the basics and quite a few luxuries to their spouses and children, and so would see a job well done. Feed and clothe your children, shelter them, as in keep a roof over their heads, educate them, and what the hell else do you want.

I always sensed as a child that my father's family were a little suspicious of, and didn't have much time for, my mother. They certainly didn't understand her, she had a calm aura about her that was foreign to what they knew, and so they couldn't identify with her. She was too civilized and soft, and beyond their experience on so many levels. She was the nurturer, certainly while all her children were very young, and they observed this, as if watching an alien in action. They knew that she was not like them. However, I sensed as a child, they wanted to be more like her; they just didn't know how. I don't imagine there were too many confidences exchanged, but she became for most of them the go to person when issues arose in their own lives. I remember one of them had a drinking problem, another an abusive home situation, or something that threw their lives upside down, and my mother was the calm talker, the one that sat with them at the kitchen table, and talked them through it, until they were ready to give it another try. Her own children were still very young at this stage, and I imagine she was in a safe and secure time of her own life, and this made it easier to offer the help. She wasn't one to gossip either, and this was probably what made her so appealing, because God knows they exchanged plenty of gossip with each other.

They watched each other like hawks, and for me, as I got older, I could easily see competition was alive and well among them, in a predatory sort of way. The interaction I had with them was minimal, a couple of times a year in passing at most. I was aware they were there and in my father's life, more than I thought of them in relation to myself. The exception for me was my Godmother, who was my father's sister, who together with her husband became my strong supporters as I moved into my early teen years and beyond. They had a restaurant on the town's main square, and I was always welcome there and treated to whatever I wanted. I felt safe with them, and their joking style of interaction was a lot of fun.

My father's mother was sharp and intelligent; she was an excellent businesswoman. She had to be; she in essence had no husband and had to raise eight children by herself. But she was cold, and a tough person to like, forget love. My father was very connected to his mother, I can't say close because that would imply some sort of emotional or affectionate connection, which I never saw, but he needed her approval long after he was married and raising children himself. Daily, till the day she died, he delivered her dinner to her at her house, a dinner cooked, I might add, by my mother, and he never saw anything unusual in this arrangement. Apart from dinner delivery, he would pop in to see her at other times during the day; she lived in town, easy access. Looking back, I would say she had many roles she played in his life. I don't imagine many decisions were made without consulting her, and even decisions already made would need the requisite pat on the back for approval. Beyond knowing that she and my mother were not close and had very little in common, and this purely from a child's intuition, I have no idea if my mother felt any resentment. I do remember asking, on occasion, about the whereabouts of my father, and the answer would be, "where do you think", and we all knew what that meant.

My father's mother was never seen by us in the grandparent role, and that in itself speaks volumes, especially considering she lived in the same town. I have no memory of ever eating a meal at her house; in fact I could count on one hand the number of times I was ever in her house. In later years, I came to view her solely as his role model and this view allowed some forgiveness, I can't say tolerance, of his inability to be a parent beyond the scope of provider. He admired her greatly and strived to be like her.

Chapter Seven

So, when you think about this young couple's earlier lives you see that their different value systems were at odds with each other, and it was only a matter of time before they both knew it. I find it interesting that even as a child I was aware of all this, so I can't help but wonder what level of denial was going on in the adult brains around me, as we were all growing up through the various stages of childhood. By summer of 1972, when her mother died, my mother had eleven children, the eldest of whom was only sixteen, and she herself was forty-one. She had been married for seventeen years, and celebrated seventeen Christmases and other holidays at her original family home, accompanied by her husband and children. With her mother now gone, and the family dynamic about to change, some serious disconnection was about to happen. Life would never be the same.

Very early in their marriage this young couple decided to go into business for themselves. Not a surprise, given that the entrepreneurial gene was alive and well and encouraged on his side of the family. He had watched his mother take over the reins of the family and find ways to provide for her children. If there was an opportunity around the town to make money she knew about it and got to work. She was the sole person at all the dog track events, days, nights and weekends. She sold fruit, chocolate, and sandwiches. When she sold out, she packed up and went home, and restocked for the next event. She had stalls in many locations, in her own and surrounding counties. If she knew an event was on, she was there.

All of her children had jobs from a very young age. Her sons were the ones granted the honor of collecting the newspapers, fresh off the trains from Dublin and Cork, and distributing them around town. My father, during a visit to the States about five years ago, reminisced about the early 40s. He talked about how he would show up scrubbed, and in a shirt and tie, at the main hotel in the centre of town. He would be the first, I can still hear him say, "remember that, first, because we were there first, we got the job". Even though they were young, they got a reputation for themselves, of not only being presentable, but reliable, honest and punctual.

As he and his two brothers got to driving age, his mother bought a car, and voila they had a taxi business, called a hackney in those days. They worked all hours and made money. It all went into the family pot. His mother made it clear very early on that this was family money. He once told me a story of how he had worked hard at lots of different jobs and was saving his share for a car. From a very early age he was a car lover, and had his eye on a fancy spitfire coupe, that he wanted. He was close to his goal, and went to get the money from its hiding place in his room, and it was gone. His mother had taken it! He was devastated. Her control was all powerful, and while this was a hard lesson for him, he exerted the same control later in his own life with his own children.

So, when he got married, and at that point was working selling insurance, it was always the intention to open his own business; it was what he grew up knowing. He saw an opportunity for a grocery store, what we call a convenience store today, and they opened at a location close to residential areas in the town where he had grown up. They worked together and she also managed the children and the household. I remember, as young children, we ran from house to shop, right beside each other. A few years later they bought a site half way down the same street, and built a house and shop, attached. For the next fifteen years the business grew. They had expanded also, and their second location on the main Square was the town's first supermarket. It was a three story building, with the supermarket on the ground floor and offices and apartments on top. At one point they had up to 20 employees.

Chapter Eight

Their children were at various stages of school; the girls enrolled at the Ursuline Convent, and the boys at the Christian Brothers. Money seemed plentiful, and there were lots of extras, like piano lessons, elocution, sports, even trips to other European countries. For all intents and purposes, life was good. My mother was involved in the business when she had to be but she hated it. As her family grew, she was off the hook; the job of taking care of so many children was all consuming.

There were lots of family Baptisms, first Communions and Confirmations as her children grew and passed from one stage to the next. She might have had all three in the same month! It was always her job to keep the children presentable and clean. She made the school uniforms, made sure the white socks were white, and the shoes polished. She got everyone ready for the various ceremonies and made the clothes herself a lot of the time. It was a big deal for all the family to look put together and cared for, and to look prosperous and well provided for. The biggest compliment my father could receive, especially after Mass on Sunday, or after a gathering for a special event in the Cathedral, or around town, was, "aren't they a credit to you". This comment

35

based solely on appearance, thus fuelling my father's belief that appearance was all that mattered.

She had help in the house, I remember a live in housekeeper, a cleaner, and I also remember the linens/ sheets got sent out to a laundry. But even with all this help, with so many small children, it was hard to keep up. My mother always cared for the newest baby herself and tried to meet the needs of the other small children, who were ever present. She loved to cook and bake and as the family grew, the size of her pies and dishes grew to keep up. She also trained all her children, boys as well as girls, in the joys of taking care of themselves and the home. We had jobs to do and were expected to help.

With my mother, it was never a case of being watched to see if you did the job right, she would show us, and then leave us to get on with it, always appreciative of the help. As a result we were motivated to help her, saw doing something as lightening her load. She went and got her hair done every Saturday and as we got older and could be useful, we all had to help in the business or stay home and help my mother. I helped her as much as I could, just happier to stay in the home and not be in the business. I enjoyed surprising her; getting all the clothes washed and out on the line, a batch of scones made and maybe supper prepared or the kitchen floor scrubbed, all completed while she got her hair done.

I know now that being with her was calm and satisfying, and she was so appreciative of anything that helped; any job that saved her from having to fit it in to her already busy days. I remember well the times when she was pregnant, the tiredness especially, and the luxury it was to her for one of us to say, take a rest, I can do it. Keep the house going and keep whatever child/children quiet. Many times, I would bring a tray of tea up to her room, and she would say thank you, and enjoy another haven of time in the quiet, and maybe enjoy a bubble bath, as there was time yet before the business closed, and my father arrived for the evening meal.

There was no question about dinner being on the table, we all knew what time he'd be home and he was as good as a clock to tell time by, and so that's when the meal should be ready. I don't think it ever crossed his mind that she might have been up to her eyes with a sick or cranky child, or a visitor or even a leaky washing machine. Over the years, as we got older, we could never understand it; his lack of contribution with the daily chores, especially as my mother trained all her sons in the art of taking care of themselves and helping out. I think he just had no clue how much work was entailed and so had no appreciation of how his own wife spent her days. His distance from the daily routine of the household and all of us only enhanced the idea of his being apart; separate.

Chapter Nine

Their social life revolved around the Chamber Of Commerce and the Church. I have many vivid memories of my mother, all dressed up in a beautiful gown with her jewels on, and my father in a dress suit, ready to dine and dance the night away. The next morning, we gathered around the breakfast table and listened to all the fun details of their night out. My mother told us who they met, what they ate, and what music they danced to. They knew other business people and locals at these events, but this social interaction never spilled over into our home. They were never comfortable mixing one part of their lives with the other. This served to cement the idea of separation and isolation in their children's minds.

They were both excellent dancers, something all their children learned and inherited. At one point, I remember, they were also involved in Marriage Encounter, and had weekends away, a sort of extended date night. I remember on many occasions, seeing them as affectionate and caring to each other. Birthdays and anniversaries were generously celebrated. He did not skimp on gifts for her birthday, their anniversary or especially Christmas; there would be flowers and perfumes and many times a special piece of jewelry.

I remember going to the local jeweler and being given an assortment of bracelets, rings and necklaces, and bringing them to my father at his own business, and he would choose what he wanted to keep.

Every Wednesday, the early closing day for their own business, they took trips, just the two of them. He liked to take her shopping for herself, at Todds Department store in Limerick, and he would patiently sit as she was assisted with her choices and she would then model the choices for him. They also travelled abroad; Lourdes, France and Spain. All of this probably contributed to their twelve offspring, in later years, feeling a very strong division between 'them' and 'us'.

When they were off doing their own thing, we were cared for, by either the housekeeper of the time, an aunt, or ourselves as we got older. Remember, there is a twenty year age difference between the eldest and the youngest. Even though there was all this 'loving interaction', my mother did not escape the emotional abuse entirely. There were times when he could forget what they meant to each other, and leave her puzzled as a total stranger by the way he would speak to her, or he might walk away and not speak for hours. The way he would insist, that with regard to the children, his word was final. We could see this and more often than not, wondered why she didn't have more input in how she would allow someone to speak to her or indeed to her offspring.

We also figured that if we were afraid of him then she must be too. As we got older, the biggest puzzle was how he could reconcile this sort of not very nice behavior, with being in Church. I could never understand it. Finally, I have to grant that he was so far in denial, that he genuinely saw nothing wrong with anything, so saw no reason to change. The idea of providing a roof over your head and food on the table was so firmly entrenched, that he thought he was doing an amazing job. Events, in later years, would show me just how unconscious he was as a parent.

Chapter Ten

My father ran a business, but the other love of his life, as I have hinted, was being involved in the Church. He went to Mass every day. We all went to Mass on Sundays, and devotions every Sunday evening. We went to Mass every day in Lent and always attended the Retreats and Novenas.

Anything to do with the Church, he was there. Get your throat blessed for St. Blaise; get your Ash Wednesday ashes, your palm on Palm Sunday. Attend the Easter ceremonies, attend the May procession, and show up at the seminary for the first blessings of the new priests. He was there for it all, and we, as his children, also attended. All this was almost typical for life in the 60s and 70s in Ireland; the Church and Church activities still featured strongly in everyday life and the priests were the final voice in how life was lived.

The only difference for us was that my father allowed the Church events and holidays to punctuate his calendar year, and he was always on the altar; preparing it for Mass, doing the reading, giving out Communion and helping out in any and every way he saw fit. We joked among ourselves; that if he hadn't gotten married, he would have been a priest.

41

Chapter Eleven

The early 70s were prosperous and busy. My youngest brother Fintan was born in 1972; he was the eleventh child and fourth son. My beloved grandmother died later that same year; I remember being inconsolable at her funeral, knowing that for me, indeed all of us, the end of an era had arrived. My father told me that morning at the funeral, that I had to control myself, it wasn't my mother who had died and suggested I was upsetting my mother. I don't think he had any clue of how attached to her I was, and he had no understanding of the significance of the loss.

The Christmas after she died, the uncles still had us over for Christmas Day. I was invited to stay there on Christmas Eve; the uncles did Santa in the form of a giant Panda bear and lots of baby bears. It was THE most wonderful surprise. It meant so much to me to be there, and the loving remembrance of my grandmother, and the proximity to the safe place I had always had with her, helped me to deal with the loss and the changes in tradition that would soon come to be. This was our last Christmas at Kilconnell and the memories are bitter sweet. I can only imagine what the loss meant to my mother, she had lost her mother just months earlier, and now a tradition for her and her own family, was also ending.

She continued to go and visit her brothers regularly; sometimes driving over alone for an afternoon, and to this day, the remaining siblings are strongly connected. Also at this time, the relationship to the sister closest to her in age got stronger. I remember outings to her house and playing with my cousins. I guess they each needed the other, if only as a reminder of where they had come from.

Business was still booming, and it was in the early 70s that a major renovation was done to the family home. An extension was added, which included a dining room big enough for the large family, and a state of the art kitchen, with every conceivable modern convenience. The kitchen had a large picture-window looking onto the back yard. I remember a trip my parents took to find the antique table and chairs and sideboard, and how formal and grand it all looked in place, but we used it every day and it became the centre of activity. Their youngest child, not yet born, would make under that dining room table her place of comfort as a small child; if we were ever looking for her, that's where she would be. The carver chair, as it was called, became my father's throne and it was from here you got to hear about whatever misdeed had been committed that day.

Small things, like no dessert forks in place, became an example of somebody's stupidity or inability to remember what was necessary. And God forbid it was your turn to cook and something burned; one of my sisters couldn't cook to save her life, and she paid the price by being on the receiving end of a long list of reasons why she couldn't do anything right. He watched TV as he ate, and I got into the habit, as we all did, of hoping something he liked would come on; it would take his mind off us.

The sense of being on eggshells came from the sudden interrogation like questions that could be fired in your direction. I used to eat fast and get out of there as fast as possible, homework called or I was doing a job for my mother. Thinking back, the two of them spent a lot of time alone in the dining room; we all had busy going on elsewhere.

The inability to sit at a table with too many people was one of the side effects that I had to deal with, as I grew up. I had to learn and am still learning, the art of relaxation and feeling safe, to be able to sit and enjoy a meal without expecting to be verbally attacked. On the positive side I learned to move efficiently, became an expert at anticipating other people's needs, and would never forget anything as I prepared a table for a dinner party. On the more serious negative side and something that has continued as a larger than life ongoing difficulty for me, large formal gatherings put the fear of God in me, especially weddings. Even to this day and no amount of rational thought seems to help. The fear and stress, so out of proportion, has prevented me from attending many events where attendance would have brought me so much joy.

Chapter Twelve

An annual event for the family, from when we were very small, was the trip to Co. Kerry and the beach. We would head towards the sea every July 1st, and stay for the month and sometimes through the August bank holiday. This was a major mark of success for my father and everyone in town knew about these holidays. He was proud to be able to do this for his family. It started for me a major love of the sea; even today, a trip to the beach and the first glimpse of the ocean is pure ecstasy. I refer to our beach place in the States as my American version of my childhood retreat.

The day before the trip was spent packing up, we brought everything with us. My mother sat at the kitchen table and made her lists. These would be given to a staff member at our own supermarket and the boxes of supplies would be the first things in the car. My father prided himself on his expertise at packing the car; not for him the style of fling it in wherever it fits. When he was finished the job, you couldn't fit a piece of paper between anything, and nothing moved in transition. My mother packed for all of us and never forgot anything. Again, in hindsight, I am in awe. I pack for two or three of us when we travel and I always say to myself, whatever I forget, we can buy. My father expected that nothing be forgotten and my mother learned to live up to this expectation. She had it down to a fine art.

Apart from food and clothes, we packed books; enough and more for a family of readers. We took a trip to the library the day before, my mother would have called ahead and the librarian would have a stack ready for her, and all we had to do was browse and choose our own. For my mother, especially, being at the beach meant the freedom to read, and it was delicious to anticipate such pure indulgence. We couldn't wait to get started.

En route to the beach, once we had crossed into County Kerry, we would start to see hitchhikers, and my father's response was always to knock on the roof of the car, as if to say that's the only available space. I remember there were times, especially when we were younger, that a long road trip was nuts. Established habits are more easily understood from the distance of time, and I now have a better understanding of what it must have been like to have so many small children in the confines of a car. The need to keep them occupied and quiet, at least some of the time.

I have to say here, and I may say it again, and again, that I strongly believe that this many children was insanity, and there is no argument that would change this conviction. Having said that, you can't change what already is, and all twelve of us are each other's strongest supporter and defender. We share in what was, and so stand in awe of what is, and what can be, with a true understanding of the struggle.

In the car, when we heard my father bless himself, we knew that was the cue to start the rosary. We took turns with a decade and all joined in for the grand finale. For us kids, if you knew your turn to pray was coming up and you didn't feel like it, it was acceptable to each other to pretend to be asleep! And somebody else would take your turn. We also sang, ten green bottles and others in the same genre, and then when we were older, we had an Irish ballad and maybe one or two from the top ten. Even with all this ritual, there were times when all the chatter and sometimes bickering from the back seats, would drive my father crazy. He would stretch back and give whoever he felt was at fault, a wallop across the head or an arm pinch, and he was so adept at this, he could reach back to the 3rd row! Other times, he'd stop the car, and dump us all on the side of the road and drive off!

My mother was still sitting in the front seat shaking her head. Picture all these small children, standing there and wondering what to do, as we saw his car disappear up the road. We asked each other did we think he was coming back. He was usually parked up ahead and as we reloaded into the car, we were given a firm warning of, "don't make me do that again".

We always stopped for a picnic, and the places to stop were interesting, to say the least. We might be pulled up to a gate that led to somebody's farmyard, or we might be sitting at a picnic table. The food was always the same, chicken or ham sandwiches and bottles of lemonade or orange, Jersey creams or Kimberley. The journey continued, and I remember the smell of the sea in the air and we knew we had arrived. I can close my eyes and still feel it; peace and calm and an ocean just waiting for us.

We walked and swam, and played tennis and read, and generally lived active busy days with not a care in the world. This is the place where all of us children had the strongest sense of being together, with a firm feeling of unfettered freedom; just us. There were rock pools on one side of the beach that you could walk to when the tide was out, and this is where we all learned to swim. I have strong memories of early morning swims and walks along the beach with my father; both of us early risers, with the shared love of a quiet beach. We admired the early morning riders as they guided their horses to the edge of the surf.

There was an Irish college on the edge of the town that held Ceilis/Irish dances on certain nights, and these and the carnival, with its rides and slot machines, constituted our night life. We walked to the outskirts of the town and enjoyed the music and fun of these social events, polishing our dancing skills and enjoying interacting with the college's students from different parts of Ireland.

As the weekend rolled around my father returned to the business, and my older sister went with him. I, and I think all of us, breathed a sigh of relief; my mother was so much more relaxed and calm when he was gone. I'm not sure why I sensed this, we were on holiday after all and the actual way we spent the day was pretty much the same, whether or not he was there. But there was a sense of a letting up of rules and she had a way of saying yes to us; that was simply a trust- filled permission and not a granting of a major favor.

As a result, we relaxed and just were, without the confines of being on guard. This was where her own style of parenting shone; she was by herself and made up her own mind, and she didn't have the fear of being judged and found wanting. We all knew she trusted us and we never did anything to betray that trust. We appreciated the calm around her, and the peace and feeling of being ok that we had when she was the sole parent.

Chapter Thirteen

My father's style, by contrast, was suspicious and confrontational and very scary to small children. It is sad for me to observe this, because it's like an insipid, under layer of rot, under what was really a good life. It's sad to remember that feeling of pervasive uncertainty. In later years, when attempts were made by more than one of us to explain this to my father, the first words out of his mouth were always, "didn't I do this and this and this for you"; he could never understand. His mind was completely closed; he couldn't even hear you because he had tuned out. There was never any doubt that we were well provided for, that he worked hard and gave us all the opportunities that he could, and that we were indeed appreciative, but what we really wanted he couldn't give. He was not evolved or self aware; indeed would be confused by the use of these terms.

Every Saturday evening, in preparation for his return, my mother would have dinner ready, and an apple pie baked for dessert, and we would watch for the returning car. Like well trained soldiers we carried the next week's supplies in, and put them away exactly where they belonged, and then left them to themselves, to catch up. We all prayed we had done nothing wrong and that the peace of his absence would continue, even though he was back.

It was on one such weekend that something happened, that became for me one of those moments where you remember the before, and the after. It was a marking point and an ending and the point from which my own journey of extreme difficulty would begin. Of course I didn't fully comprehend it then; I felt it, but I had no way of knowing. I am also pretty sure that anyone else there wouldn't even remember the conversation, having no idea of the impact or significance. My parents had been having a discussion about some development within their business; they finished their conversation and wanted to share the news. My mother came up the stairs and told us of an opportunity; to buy the building, where the primary business was. We had always been told it wasn't possible, and I said this. I know that I was not being intentionally difficult; I remember that to me the statement was just logical. My father questioned my pride or recognition of his achievement, and continued with words to dismiss me. He was consumed with anger that seemed totally out of context and proportion. It went on and on, a flow of verbal abuse from a grown man to a child; I was shattered. Of all his children, I was the one to doubt him; there I was, putting a damper on his success.

My view of him and our interaction from that day changed. I was confused, could not understand his reaction, and I was particularly stunned by his stubborn insistence that I had said or done something wrong. I felt totally dismissed and couldn't understand why. And so it was. And life went on. And the feeling of being misunderstood stayed with me, and it was all I could do to just be. My father had no clue how powerful his words could be; how hurtful this situation had been for me. My sense of loss was overpowering. As a result of this experience, the foundation for the uncertainty that would continue to frame my thoughts was firmly put in place.

Before this happened I idolized him. Even though I didn't care too much for the family he came from, I never thought of him as one of them; I saw him as an example of what they might aspire to. Especially as he was married to my mother, and that softer gentler approach was right in his own house. Little did I know then, but his influence, being of the bullying kind, would erase hers, and as the years went by and more of her children grew up, she would come to be viewed as inept, or as a passive bystander. I moved through my last few years in Secondary/High school with extreme difficulty. There continued the underlying sense of loss and confusion, and I had a hard time being physically safe anywhere. I felt confined, constantly wondering if I needed to get away.

There was one teacher/nun, who was always available for me, but I was too embarrassed to tell her what the real problem was. I don't think I could have verbalized it at that point in any event. I think she thought that my anxiety was about deciding what to do after high school. I do think, though, that even that one person showing genuine concern, helped me to hang on, and have a belief that somehow it would all be ok. My balance was off and I was unsure of my place. I struggled through and in my final year decided to enter the convent.

It is interesting to note here, that the top four children all tried religious orders as a way of life. Hard not to read further into that, given that we used to joke that my father might have been a priest, and the central part the established church played in his life. The irony of what parents unwittingly subject their children to, as their children crave acceptance.

Chapter Fourteen

Catholic priest at this time, over the two year time frame when I considered the convent as a possible vocation, offered to guide me through the process, and be a sort of religious advisor/counselor. He showed up often at our house, at different times during the day or after the evening meal. He was shown into the front room, and we were given total privacy, out of respect for his position in the church. This was the 70s, still a time when clergy were held in high esteem, operating on a different plane to the rest of us. That would change of course, in the next decade, as a growing number of informed and evolved Irish Catholics owned their responsibility for their own faith and activity within the established Church, and found a voice strong enough to be heard over the dominant clerics.

For now and for me, I was trapped by this ready acceptance. One of my siblings would bring a tray with tea and knock first, and it was through this consideration for him that I was unwittingly placed in harm's way. He had no fears of being disturbed. His interaction was totally inappropriate. He knew I was a young sixteen year old, too trusting, naïve and inexperienced. His conversation totally confused me, one time he told me not to move my face as he stood in front of me; he wanted to show me what to do and how to behave so that I would be ready for a boyfriend, something he thought a good idea to aid my decision about my life's direction. I asked myself if this was the norm and wondered if perhaps he had a genuine reason for this approach. During one of his visits, my sister walked in without knocking, and I can still see the question written on her face, as her glance moved from one to the other. I mentioned to my mother that his favorite phrase was, "Mum's the word", and asked her what that meant. She explained it to me and I saw a puzzled look on her face, but neither of us said anything further.

He continued his interest even at school; he had an amazing ability to be on his best behavior and put on what I came to see as his social face, and continue talking as if we had been having a regular conversation, if anyone showed up. All this nonsense, under the guise of spiritual direction, and I only ended up feeling more inept and confused. The older wiser me, now knows, that he had no business guiding anyone, anywhere; his only qualification being a clerical collar around his neck.

It was a very difficult time for me, I felt that I had no one to turn to, but also, that I had no clue what I really wanted to do or what direction my life might take. While there were so many incidents for me, at this time, that obviously pointed to my not being ok; leaving a classroom abruptly, walking out of the school before the day was over, or reluctant to leave at the end of the day, not a single person in my life had the skills to try and help me figure it out. Part of me was puzzled, I was sure it was obvious to everyone that something must have happened, and they just chose not to talk about it. The overall feeling, for me, was of having been let down.

The previous incident with my father, and the alienation I felt within that relationship, only compounded my sense of being adrift. This priest knows that his behavior was inappropriate, even though I never saw the need to go and confront him. My life and healing took me totally away, and the idea of returning wouldn't come for several years. I think my sense of being at the mercy of this authority figure stemmed from a reluctance to shatter my father's image of his beloved Church. Years later, I did some research on the priest's whereabouts, and learned that he was in an administrative job for the diocese, and no longer dealt with children, young adults or any lay people but his fellow priests.

At one point, about twenty years after I had left Ireland, when it was known that a priest of the diocese was being brought up on sexual abuse charges and inappropriate behavior, speculation abounded. I suggested his name to my father, and he was shocked and utterly ready to defend the guy. I found this interesting, did he not question why I would suggest someone, with whom he knew I had my own history; a person he knew to have been in a position of trust. Would he think to take it a step further and wonder if there was something his daughter was trying to share?

I felt betrayed a second time, and I remember wondering how he could be so blind. For my father, what was seen to be was paramount; he didn't know any better, it was how he was raised himself. I don't think he could have handled the truth, even if it had been more openly discussed. Don't rock the boat. Because of that strong conviction, there was always the reminder that what happened inside the four walls of the house stayed there. We all had a sense of being removed from the world outside, and this was encouraged, enforced. For that reason, it was years before I opened up about my experiences, and years before I understood my own feelings of guilt and inadequacy.

Chapter Fifteen

My father ran a tight ship, and we knew we were on an island, of sorts. By that I mean unreachable; afloat on our own, no strangers, meaning anyone outside the family, (twelve kids and two parents) may enter. The doorbell might ring and there was a feeling of invasion, being seen doing something you weren't supposed to be doing, somebody being there who didn't belong; wasn't invited. All this contributed to my sense of secrecy, something to cover up, to bring shame. I couldn't have verbalized any of this at the time, it just was.

Obviously there were visitors to the home, invited, and so expected, and then welcomed. Even relatives were encouraged to call before a visit, and never show up unannounced. This was unusual for that time, as, culturally, family and friends were used to just dropping by. My mother's family, especially, found it odd. Anyone who showed up unannounced didn't do it a second time, being deterred by the chilly reception they got.

In the early years of the business, a tradition was established that every year on the anniversary, a Mass was held on the premises, and afterwards the priest was invited to the house for breakfast. All the staff celebrated with lunch in a local hotel. I remember some years the Mass and the lunch were at our house, and it all went off smoothly, again this was planned and my father, especially, was in his element as the cordial host.

This event reinforced our sense of a public façade, if it looks great it is great, no questions asked. On more than one occasion, the priest who was my self- appointed spiritual director was the officiator of the event, compounding my sense of invasion, and doubting the safety of my own home. I was more than aware of my growing doubts and difficulties; I knew that refuge had to be found elsewhere. It took me a little longer to figure out how to achieve this.

Perceived reality and actual reality allowed the confusion to mount, and there was a pervasive sense of being stuck. I was also becoming increasingly aware of the impact of this family lifestyle on all the other young psyches running around; I was not the only one suffering consequences. We knew this was not ok, but we never really verbalized it; too young yet to have mastered the courage, wisdom or vocabulary, until years later.

Chapter Sixteen

My father's need for control was all over the place, and we learned to do everything fast and well. Did he think he was raising efficient kids to become efficient adults? I look back on it now and I shake my head, both in bewilderment and sadness. If he wanted you to vacuum the carpet, it was well known among ourselves to look for his hidden treasures. He would ask when you were done, if you were sure, and then march you in to show you where he had hidden a piece of paper or anything, and you missed it; so guess you didn't do such a good job after all. You knew what to do and that's what you did, perfectly, or you were a total idiot.

All this did was encourage us to question how we were doing anything and look around in uncertainty. As time went on, I figured out for myself, that all of this had nothing to do with a clean carpet or clean anything, and all to do with his instilling the idea that he knew more than any of us, and that we could never match up. As we got older, we wondered why my mother didn't intervene. I think she knew that she couldn't change him; she also knew from her own experience, that if questioned, he would turn the power of his words on her. Was she in a catch twenty-two?

Another issue that was huge for him was punctuality. He was a rigid time keeper, and expected no less of us, or by God you would pay the price.

Also, if he thought you were lying to him, or hadn't fully answered his questions or were even by a look, being disrespectful, then you had it coming, asking for it. If it was in the days before he started riding horses, and had a crop handy, you would meet your fate with a heater stick, a three dimensional, twenty inch piece of wood that became a tool for his temper. He would end up breaking it over whichever child was the perceived culprit. Afterwards, we all had to pray; to ask for forgiveness for making him lose his temper. Corporal punishment was alive and well, and I have no doubt that there was a very valid case for child abuse charges. He was protected by the, 'inside these four walls' etc., and everybody kept their mouths shut. It was also a time when this sort of behavior might have been frowned upon, but the time of its being considered child abuse was yet to come. He himself probably justified it by telling himself he was a good father, and needed to show his children the error of their ways.

My brothers, especially, had it hard, and as my younger sisters grew into their teens, their every action and natural push toward independence was seen as a threat to his authority. We helped each other though, and after I had left the convent; realizing it was not for me and was living away and studying, I would return to take my sisters out. We would go for a drive or some other activity, to get out of the house, and an opportunity to vent. We indulged in simple pleasures; a movie, an ice-cream or a drive. We were reassuring each other that the insanity was still, thank God, inside those four walls, and outside of them escape awaited us, normalcy and sanity was possible.

My mother continues quietly in the background, no obvious signs have appeared yet, at least that she can't avoid seeing, of the adverse effects of such treatment of children and young people, so she hasn't been forced yet to take a closer look. What was she thinking? I imagine she was overwhelmed. So many children at so many different phases of development, and your partner a control freak with a serious temper; a person who always sees everything in relation to himself. I can see her plodding along and keeping the physical needs of her children met. Beyond that, she was stumped. As the years were passing, I think she tried to find ways to compensate but there was nothing she could do; either to fix it or to make it ok to do nothing. In years to come, her children would wonder at her competence in the mother role, as she would herself.

Chapter **Seventeen**

If I step aside here, for a moment, and see this from the perspective of someone outside the family, the angle change tells a whole different story. What they see is not completely false, just not the whole story. The appearance of a well cared for, well educated family was carefully presented, and if you believed what you saw, there was no need to question it. It's not like there was a major cover up going on; it was more a case of being ashamed and mortified and once the front door of the house closed behind you, you engaged fully with the outside world. We were all too young anyway, to clarify any of the feelings in a coherent way.

By fully engaged I mean having a regular school life, sports, friends etc. Only one close friend, from my Secondary/High school days, would have had any idea of a problem; she obviously knew of my developing difficulties in social situations, and knew something was not ok, but she had no idea of the truth until years later. There was so much normal that was mixed in with the not so normal. This only heightened the sense of uncertainty.

I remember lots of events, the natural markers in a child's life, when we had friends over and had an amazing time.

All of my friends thought my father was great; funny, witty, and sociable. Birthdays were celebrated, and parties were held with friends, and there was lots of effort put into them. I remember picnics and movie parties, and having groups of friends come for dinner and a sleepover. After all of these events, my father would pile me and all my friends, into his custom ordered Peugeot with three rows of seats, (the pride of his life!) and drop everyone home. Along the way there would be joking and laughing, and in these situations he was anyone's dad. These interims, for me, allowed a tiny window to stay open; where I would continue to be optimistic about a possible relationship and perhaps hopeful that he could be trusted to stay consistent.

Events at home, however, allowed the confusion to grow. The contrast between how we felt and how other people viewed him became more pronounced. A child starts to question the validity of their own observations, and when you cannot clearly understand what is in front of you, you begin to doubt your own sense of perception. This sets the stage for crippling self- doubt, and it grows until you are at the point where you don't even remember what confused you in the first place.

The same normalcy applied to Christmas, we celebrated in huge style. Christmas Eve for all of us was magical, as we set up the decorations and put the finishing touches on the tree. We gathered for Midnight Mass in the Cathedral, all of us dressed in our beautiful new clothes. Afterwards, we returned home for tea and the cutting of the Christmas cake, and then off to bed to await Santa. We always exchanged gifts with each other, and my parents not only did Santa, but also gave each child an individual gift, from themselves. I remember waking up on Christmas morning, and being almost sick with anticipation and feeling for the stocking; if it was bulky Santa had arrived, if empty, go back to sleep. And then the mad rush to go downstairs and find the real gifts.

There were bikes and rocking horses, doll houses and tricycles, dolls and guns, train sets, teddy bears and whatever else we had asked for, in our letters mailed a month prior. Each of us always got an annual, a selection box and a surprise, on top of all the other gifts. Picture the scene with all these kids let loose, in a living room that resembled a toy store. I remember some of us, after some time spent checking out the gifts downstairs, would return to our rooms, to read the new annuals or books and eat candy. I remember dragging stuff up to my parent's bedroom; to show them what Santa had brought.

As we got older and increased in number, they had to get creative with keeping it all hidden. Years later, we learned that a builder's supplier business, across the street, used to store it all in their warehouse, and drag it over on Christmas Eve, after we had gone to sleep. When I think of it now, they were amazingly generous and must have spent a small fortune. Not surprisingly, Christmas remains the most important holiday to celebrate, and here I find myself, years later, trying to recreate for my family the Christmas that I grew up with.

Around noon, we would gather our favorite new toys, pack up the car and head to my Grandparents' farm, for the Christmas dinner. As we drove up the lane off the main road, we could smell the turkey and couldn't wait to sit around the farmhouse table for the feast. There was turkey and stuffing, ham, carrots and parsnips mixed together, sprouts, potatoes and gravy. All this followed by plum pudding with trifle, fruit and whipped cream. I feel stuffed just thinking about

it. After the meal, we would pull crackers, don our party
hats and eat chocolate. I remember games of checkers with
my Uncle Thomas, followed by card games and whatever
new games we might have gotten as gifts.

My grandmother would have picked up something small
for each of us; a game, a toy car, or a small doll. One year,
I got a cardboard doll that came with different outfits that
you had to cut out, and I remember she came with three
different heads, so that you could switch around her hair
color. I kept it safely in a box for years. By early evening,
when we were ready to eat again, there was cold turkey
with homemade bread, and then, the pièce de résistance,
remembered so vividly; the Christmas cake.

Hours later, the day would draw to a close and we
reluctantly gathered our stuff and packed up the car, for
the drive home. We inevitably fell asleep, and I remember
being comforted only by the fact that my grandparents were
coming to our house the next day, traditionally celebrated
in Ireland as St. Stephen's day.

Every year since, it doesn't matter what's on the menu
for dinner, I have to have my Christmas cake. With this
tradition, I am transported back to my grandparents' farm.
One Christmas, in the United States, I made six of them, and
sent them off in the mail for siblings and friends. All living in
other States, but just as happy as me to have the opportunity
to blend the old with the new, and to have a little bit of
home as part of their holiday celebration. The screams of joy
and remembrance will echo in my ears forever!!

Chapter Eighteen

Recently, my best friend since school reminded me that my father even gave her some driving lessons. He was the affable friend's father, helping out. This conversation brought back the memory of his teaching me to drive. Hours spent driving around country roads, and up over the railway bridge, to stop half way to learn how to control the car on the hill; with the hand brake and the clutch. If I heard, "don't let her roll back", once, I heard it a hundred times. He spent hours teaching me to reverse into a parking spot, and how to do a three point turn. And he still wasn't done. I had to know about the tire pressure, and the oil level and general maintenance for the vehicle. I passed my test on the first round, and was proud to say it was because he taught me. When I bought my first car he was there to help, to advise so I didn't get a lemon, as he was for all my siblings, if asked.

This is what makes the reality so much harder. It could have been so different. So much pain and self-torture for me and other issues for my siblings, could have been avoided. The insidious symptoms of what happened to us are so much harder for other people to understand, than say a burn or a broken nose; because they can't be seen, the injuries to a child's psyche are not so easily healed. Do the good memories balance the not so good? Unfortunately they do not; there will always be an overwhelming appreciation for the generosity, but the struggle with difficulties, unnecessarily placed on our lives, will continue. There is some feeling of comfort from knowing a lack of intention, and this helps the instinct toward forgiveness.

Even living away and trying to live a productive life, studying and teaching some classes, I still trailed or acted as a magnet for the not so healthy stuff I thought I had left behind. The first time I called and said I wouldn't be home for the weekend, I was told, if so, don't bother coming here ever again. I was shocked, and I remember thinking that being older, away and self sufficient made no difference. His need for control was still there. I didn't actually go home that weekend and paid the price until forgiveness was granted. Each time something like this happened it was like another blow. I felt pulled in a hundred different ways, and like there was a permanent puzzle in front of me, that I could never figure out. I can still feel physically the reaction I would have, debilitated, as if punched and frail.

When I was twenty, the youngest child at home was two, and there were six others, all the way up to seventeen. So I was grown and away, while the next generation within the same family was just starting; coming face to face with their confusion and figuring out their own survival skills. For this second group of children, life was even more difficult; as business challenges were cropping up because of the economy. This caused a high level of anxiety, and my father's intolerance of independent thinking outside himself compounded his feeling of losing control. I remember many phone calls from younger siblings, as they tried to understand the confines of home, and all I could do was offer verbal consolation and the offer of a place to stay for a weekend break.

We did this sort of back up support all the time. They could come and vent, and be reassured, and then be ok to go back. We spent a lot of time together and I guess that still follows today, with all the siblings/children getting together on a regular basis, or continuing the connection with long inter State or Trans- Atlantic phone calls. At one time, there were eight of us living in the United States, and the hint that there was another one about to arrive would always start with the sentence, "I have to get away from here". I think we all felt the need to establish ourselves, and feel strong, away from the home base.

The couple who started their business, and their family, with so much optimism or foolish hope, now found themselves surrounded by people of all ages, and they had no idea how to do the job. I think they forgot that this was the end result, small babies and small children do grow into adults, whether you are conscious of it or not. And you may impose your will and expectations as strongly as you choose, but they will be free thinkers one day, and have the right to react and move on, out, or up, and your days of control are over.

How I wish it had been all as simple as moving out. The baggage came too. The impact of the denying of parental acceptance and love was starting to manifest itself. For each of their children it manifested itself in different ways, but each would have their struggles. I was crippled with insecurities and anxiety; couldn't function on some very basic levels. But I tried hard to continue and live some semblance of a normal life.

On visits back, I would continue to pick my mother up,

and go with her to visit her family. This was a very good thing for me, a way to still feel the connection to my mother's family, and allow myself to remember what I had had there. I think on some level it gave me the positive identity I needed. I admired all of her siblings so much and greatly appreciated the open honest welcome to their homes; it was so relaxing for me. To this day, my mother's two siblings still living are always included in my visits home.

Interestingly, I was able to separate my mother from the sadness that I was working through. I never felt the same sense of outrage with her. I thought of her as a pacifist, and someone who continued to provide for the physical needs of her children, even though she must have been aware, not just of what was going on, but also of the future consequences. My sisters and I are strong, strong women, admittedly hard earned, and perhaps this is our reaction to her perceived pacifism. There were times when she followed her own maternal instinct and helped us out, but she always felt the need to do this in secret; behind my father's back. She would give one of my younger sisters the money for a weekend with one of the older ones, or she would put gas money in your hand after a visit. I remember an incident; one of my brothers had been estranged and away in another country for a couple of years. On his return, he was not made especially welcome by my father, being seen as too independent in making decisions on his own. As he left the house, my mother followed him to the front door, and put a wrapped home- made fruit cake into his hands; as if this was enough to compensate for the chilly reception. We understood what she was doing; her way of showing love might have fallen short of what could really help or what we needed, but we knew it came from good intention.

Chapter Nineteen

I continued to study, took exams, had a job teaching to support myself, and had the sense of family I needed from my siblings. In the early 80s, I was forced to acknowledge the serious issues in many aspects of my life. Social situations were beyond me...every moment of every day was a thinking event that left me exhausted. There was no continuity in my day; every little sub section of time, as I saw it, sucking the life out of me.

Teaching a class, which I loved, I would find myself crippled with uncertainty; times when I couldn't do it. I just walked away. The panic started to show up all over the place, and I couldn't find a way to resolve it. I felt claustrophobic in supermarkets, churches and anywhere public. I would try hard to talk myself through it, and afterwards I would feel an intense sense of failure, as I could see no hope of it getting any better or easier.

I started to relieve the pain and stress physically, by self-injury, with the help of a very sharp carving knife. I didn't know how else to cope, and I ended up needing stitches over and over. But in some strange way, it helped; the broken bleeding skin was a physical tangible sign of my pain. Even though, for a long time, I was the only one to see it. I kept the scars covered and no one knew. It didn't matter how many times I put myself through this, I couldn't stop. I remember those days and nights of utter helplessness, and the only relief I could give myself was self inflicted injury. I needed a touchable something to give credence to the knowledge that something was not ok.

Oddly, the work day was easier when I had self inflicted injuries causing physical pain. It was almost as if I was coping, and the cuts were a reminder of the reality with which I lived, always present under the façade of my day. There was a comfort in knowing that I was punishing myself. I felt I must have done something, to warrant having been treated this way, and also feeling this way. I reached a point though, when it took too much effort to continue this way of living; I knew I needed help.

Divine providence intervened, and I found the doctor who would save my life, and guide me through all of this. He would help me to put my life in a place where it could be valued and for me worth living. This was the early 80s, and I actually gave up my job, suspended my financial commitments, and moved to Dublin where he was based. Was this extreme? It was very extreme, but a strong indication of how desperate I was.

This doctor made himself available to me 24/7, and God knows I tested him, and he always came through. His office became a safe place for me to go. From the get go, without knowing any of the details of my story, he assured me of the safety of this process, his own ethics, and how he himself was without judgment. I knew from the first time talking with him that here was the help I needed.

Three of my siblings, working in Dublin, were living in a house in Sandymount, a Dublin suburb, and agreed to my moving in. I would see my doctor three times or more every week; and hopefully solve some conflicts, within and without. The decision to get help was enough for me to start feeling better. It was hard and it was easy. I talked and he listened. He heard it all, even what I didn't have the words to say. These sessions punctuated my week. I thought about the one I had just attended, and the next one, and in between I wrote; pages and pages of words for all the pain and confusion.

In time, I began to feel better, to gain some understanding and forgive myself and to understand that I really wasn't the one at fault. There were emergencies, times when I thought I couldn't go on and would relapse to the comfort of the cutting. Once, I even wrote Goodbye letters to my parents, trying to explain how I felt. I wanted to die and be done with it all. They didn't even acknowledge getting my letters, continuing in the mode of denial. It was terrifying to sit alone in a house and remember all the sadness, and to feel better just by contemplating what I could do with a knife. I felt isolated, and yet I felt that my situation made perfect sense, and that all of my siblings and close friends would understand.

I saw the inside walls of a Dublin Hospital as I came for emergency visits, and went through days and weeks as if in a fog. It became part of my coping norm. I never wanted to be admitted, that would be beyond frightening. I needed to believe in the process of one on one therapy and this was my lifeline. I never considered medication of any sort, I felt it was too risky and I didn't want a crutch, I wanted a cure. This doctor stayed with me through it all; always giving me the option of talking or writing, and his time, understanding, and empathy gave me back my life.

Chapter Twenty

My parents had no involvement in any of this; my father never referred to it, acted like it never happened. My mother at least talked to me on the phone, and even once asked to see the cuts, recently stitched and bandaged. I never showed them to her, it was enough that she had asked. For me, an acknowledgement of what was going on, and the pain I was in. I can still see her sitting on the couch crying, asking if there was anything she could do. At the time, part of me felt that she was a poor excuse for a mother, and I felt she was in denial of the why and how that it had happened.

I could see too, on my fleeting visits home to visit my younger siblings, the empathy and sorrow they felt on my behalf. They were aware of my struggle, there were times when I had relied on a younger sibling to talk to, too young and stupid myself to realize that this was so irresponsible. But even that level of being accountable was impossible. I was in such a state of pain, and just barely hanging on, that I couldn't think about anyone else. Looking back, I give myself credit for searching out some help, and for staying with the treatment, recognizing that it was the only way to escape all the darkness and pain. On some level, I knew, difficult as it was to live through, this was the only way.

In later years, I understood that my father's personality totally overpowered my mother, and she could only be strong away from him. If we doubted ourselves, just from our interaction with him, perhaps she did also. I can also see, from this distance, that her confusion surely matched ours. I remember times when, if she didn't support his view or opinion, he could disappear; gone in his car and wouldn't reappear for hours. The next day, it was life as usual. So juvenile, but there wasn't a thing anyone could do. He was so not in touch with his own emotions, and it would only create further heartache to have a dialogue about it.

At various times some of us tried to bring in another adult, a family friend, but as we tried to explain the problem we were dismissed. His public image was so strong, and so firmly in place; he was the responsible father of twelve, good husband, good provider and business man, strong Church attendee and beyond. Who did we think we were to even hint at some type of abusive parental control? He was so involved in the good works of the community also; various charities he contributed to, and there were many families he would have helped out in hard times. This was not the profile of someone playing around with his children's minds.

As adults, we moved on, those who acknowledged that they needed to, found help, and in time, distance healed. My own treatment in Dublin continued for years until I started to feel better and feel able to live beyond this cocoon that was the doctor's office. While I was still seeing him, I started to teach again part-time, and this allowed for a vision of a life worth the effort. As the summer of '87 approached, I knew I would have to leave, and try and start my life over somewhere else. If I was going to continue in the vein of recovery, and believe the goodness in myself acknowledged in therapy, I needed to go somewhere new.

I was not the first one of my family to consider a change of location; other siblings had gone before me. I decided to try for a visa and go to the United States. I had no money, but I was so motivated and determined, I knew I would find a way. I remember going to a branch of a bank in Dublin and asking for a loan to finance the move; at the end of the interview with the manager I said, "if you say no to this, the no will be so big, you could stand it up on your desk." He gave me the loan, and I knew that I would pay off every penny as fast as possible, because I was so grateful for the chance. I went to the U.S. Embassy and got all the paperwork in order, backed up my visa request with letters of recommendation, and waited.

I booked a flight and packed up my stuff, the only items of any real value that I wanted to take with me were my photo albums. I arranged to meet and say goodbye to my close friends, none of whom was surprised. It's ironic to remember that when all of my planning was going on, my parents were in the States on vacation. They were totally oblivious to the fact that I had come so close to ending my own life or that I was now in the throes of finding a way to salvage it.

Saying goodbye to my doctor was the most difficult; he was my guide from there to here, my guide as I left the past and moved to the future. I felt a connection to him that I didn't yet feel strong enough to do without, but we agreed to keep in contact, and off I went. I was desperate to get away, could no longer live where it had all happened, and knew that I at least deserved the possibility of trying to start over. I would join my siblings in the United States and try my hardest to find a life worth living.

I had no idea then, but it would be twelve years! before I returned to Ireland.

Chapter Twenty-One

In 1986, one of my sisters got married, and she and her husband moved to live in the States. Another sister followed shortly after. A brother was next, and then another younger sister, and then me. So, I was the fifth in my family to choose the U.S. as an adopted home. The fifth to get on a plane and say, "thank you God", for the luxury of an escape and the chance to start over. I remember the actual trip as if it were just yesterday; I was so full of relief and gratitude for the opportunity. I was going toward, not leaving, and I think that set the tone for the next couple of months, until I found my footing.

I met my brother in JFK Airport, New York; he had lived here for over a year working in the computer programming field. This was a short visit with him, as I planned to continue north and stay with my married sister, and possibly settle close by. He was full of tips and ideas for me, and as he guided me to the correct terminal for the domestic flight, I handed over his goodies from Ireland; the requisite rashers and sausages. Those were the days when you were still allowed to bring them in. We knew we would keep in touch by phone, and see each other soon, now that we were again living in the same country.

I remember the overpowering heat; it was over 100degrees, with high humidity. When I walked out of the airport it felt like someone had opened the oven door, the heat just slapped you in the face. It was gross and I was sure it was a fluke; something weird going on to cause such intense weather. But no, over time I came to realize, that heat and humidity go hand in hand with the words, 'American summer'. At the airport, I had just come through baggage claim when I spotted my sister. It was so great to see her. The reunion was amazing; I met my nephew for the first time, only a couple of months old. I was happy to be there.

Their house was on a quiet street, walking distance from shops, and for the first few days we stayed close to home, catching up. My sister was only twenty-one years old, and here she was, married with a baby. She and her husband were settled in this northern State, living close to her husband's relatives; she too loved the anonymity of her new beginning. We enjoyed our time together, and I enjoyed spending time with my nephew.

After about four/five weeks though, I knew that this area of the States was not going to work for me. I continued to be plagued with uncertainty and anxiety, and still felt I was floating with no anchor in sight. My sister was too young and too inexperienced herself to be able to offer me any empathy or support, and I found it difficult to be a part of her life. I had no luck with a job, and I found the environment too cold and industrial, so I contacted my brother and we came to an agreement that I would try his location instead. This turned out to be the best possible decision.

My flight landed on a Saturday afternoon, and just driving from the airport I began to feel better. It wasn't called the Garden State for nothing. Trees and shrubs, flowers and plants were everywhere; it was lush and green and felt like home. I stayed with my brother for the first few days and got used to my new State. The only tough adjustment was the mosquitoes! As we all sat outside enjoying a barbecue one evening, I got more than my share of bites. We all thought nothing of it, until the following morning, when my legs and my face were badly swollen. My brother brought me to his GP, Dr. Silverman, (now deceased but lovingly remembered) who kindly agreed to see us immediately. Turns out I was having an allergic reaction, and for the next six months, I would carry an auto injector with me; to give myself a shot whenever I got bitten. This was another introduction to a person who became influential in my life, only of course I didn't know it then. Our paths would cross again, and he would be a source of reassurance and guidance as difficult medical issues arose.

I already had job interviews lined up for the following week, which allowed me to consider that I was doing what was needed toward establishing a productive life. I slept like a baby that night; some part of me knowing that it was all going to be fine. My brother was involved with the Irish community near his home, and I fell into the lifestyle and felt very comfortable. It was the ideal way to slowly acclimate to this new country; I needed the bridge this represented to get me over the jump from Ireland to the States.

I got a job, in a town about twenty minutes drive from where my brother lived. Again the angels were guiding me. I met an Irish girl who had worked there for the summer; she was returning to Ireland and she needed a replacement. Someone she could guide and help settle in before it was time for her to leave. She already knew my brother and that was how we met. I went to check it out and voila! Another very important person enters my life.

I remember walking around the block with him, chatting and telling him about myself. He was also Irish, and oddly enough his parents had lived in the same town that I came from, back in Ireland. Was this divine intervention guiding me? He described his daughter, told me that his wife had died, and said basically that he was fairly laid back and would I like to give it a try. He worked in New York, a thirty minute bus ride away, and his top priority was his daughter and her well being. As we talked, we sort of had a little hint, even then, of the friends we would become. His daughter, Jennifer, was nine years old, had cystic fibrosis and he needed someone to do her therapy, take care of her etc etc...and I got the job.

I told him later, that I also wanted to keep teaching, maybe do some substitute teaching, and he agreed. It was a given that we had an understanding here, Jennifer would be my top priority and whatever else I wanted to fit in was fine. I had my own apartment at the top of the house which was perfect for me, as I had been used to independence.

I can still see myself looking out the window that first day, looking out at the tree lined streets and the green lawns, and feeling like I should pinch myself; it was all too good to be true. I felt safe and at peace and hard though it is to believe, I felt like I had come home. There was an immediate sense of belonging and feeling this is where I am meant to be. Of course I had no way of fully knowing it then, but he and his daughter would become so important in my life; have front row seats in all the events that would happen from then on.

Chapter Twenty-Two

There was no settling in period; from day one, all three of us lived at #91, with a sense of well being, and I had no doubt that I was where I belonged. The right fit at the right time. Daily life no longer felt so hard, I loved the structure of Jennifer's day, and enjoyed our time as we got to know each other. She was a fun open kid, and her father's daughter; fun to be with and happy to go along with whatever plans were in place for the day. She had inherited his Irish wit and quick retort and we had some fun verbal exchanges.

The day started with the three of us having breakfast, her Dad would leave for the city, and I would take her to school. During her absence I would do household stuff, food shopping and cooking. I slowly felt more comfortable bringing my own stamp to this new life; as I felt more at home, I made it home. I would bake a pie or a cake as a special after school treat, make Irish stew for dinner. I would help Jennifer with homework, and together we brought fun and enjoyment into the day, and it became the norm. On days that she was off school, we slept late, did her therapy, and over breakfast planned our excursions.

She was also a booklover, and she brought me to the

library and the bookstore. She was a guide in the town where she herself had always lived, and she and I made it mine together. She was an excellent student; we had great discussions and debates as she did projects and homework assignments. We played board games, watched TV movies, and had afternoon tea. Sometimes her Dad had out of town trips, and for both of us it became like a sleepover. We would do all her therapy first, drive to McDonald's for fries and Burger king for the chicken sandwich. She loved that I would do that; two stops just to get exactly what we loved. We would return home and maybe bake, and I taught her to be a snob about Irish flour and other ingredients. She got to the point of saying, "we can't make a cake, because we have no Irish flour".

Many nights, we played hide and seek, running round the house in search of each other. Her favorite spot to hide was the coat closet in the downstairs powder room, and over and over I would be surprised to discover her, and always she would scream in fright. She was so much fun; happy and so appreciative of her life and everyone in it. She attended a local Catholic private school, and so for me her school had something of the familiar about it, and echoes of my own experience.

There were competitions, held annually, among the students for St. Patrick's Day and it became a point of honor to win, year after year. When I look back at the photos, I think she must have really loved me; some of the tri color concoctions I came up with, and dare I admit it, readily coerced her into wearing. And one year we hauled a giant stuffed leprechaun (And I mean giant!) down from the attic, and she hauled him off as a prop. I took her to doctor appointments and dentist appointments, and gradually, we blended the imposition of her cystic fibrosis with living and every possible fun activity, and we lived and loved life.

I slowly relaxed and started to see the possibilities of a life free of stress. We moved beyond the town and drove to explore Bear Mountain, with music blaring in the car, and picnics when we got there. We toured New Rochelle, New York City and the Jersey shore. I was alive and happy to be!

She was energetic and hardy, and I, over time, learned to listen to her symptomatic cough to gauge how she was doing. She went to the hospital once a year, usually at Easter time, and spent a week getting more concentrated therapy to keep her healthy. I would go and see her there every afternoon, and she would entertain me with the stories going on round her, while we both scoffed Irish candy. The nurses loved her; so present and entertaining and not once was she a whiner or a complainer. And she was a kid; delving into her Easter basket to discover if her favorite Starburst had been remembered, and loving that I introduced her to the Irish tradition of boxed chocolate eggs. My family and friends were always welcome at 91; Jennifer loved the craziness of my large family, being an only child herself. It was a way for all of us to get to know each other, and savor the common bond of being Irish. Jennifer loved all the attention and being included, especially when a package for me arrived from Ireland and there was one included for her. She wasn't just my job; she was very much a central part of my life.

Interaction with her Dad was calm and enjoyable; he was a straight talker, mixed up sometimes with his playful way of speech. The Irish charm mixed in with his command of English. We both had considerable respect for each other, felt rather than spoken. The old, 'actions speak louder than words,' I guess. He was kind and considerate, and any discussion about the household or Jennifer was done in a conversational way. Such a novel experience for me and such a lesson too. I observed, mostly in an unconscious way, his interaction with his child. He was such a great Dad, and I got such a kick seeing them bounce off each other, both intending to give as good as they got.

They spent every weekend, mostly just the two of them, but sometimes their family and friends joined them. As she got older, they went to movies and dinner, and then, as she moved into her teens, he became the chauffeur and confidant. It was such a learning experience for me on so many levels, to see this father interact with this daughter, and to see how it could be, and when they come to mind today it all just brings a smile to my face, and it is one of my greatest blessings to have been a part of it.

Chapter Twenty-Three

My brother brought me along to an Irish club get together one weekend, there was Irish food, dancing and of course, chat. This became a major part of my social life. Irish Americans welcoming all of us from home, delighted with everything and anything we did. Every year, adult Irish language classes were held, and my first year there they were short a teacher and I stepped in to fill the gap. I had about twenty in my group, a mixed bunch; elementary teachers, retired people, a Jesuit priest (who four years later would concelebrate my wedding mass!) and a few young Irish American couples wanting to rekindle their love of Ireland and all things Irish. It renewed my love of the language, and gave me a wonderfully entertaining outlet for all that was Home!

It is true that for all Irish people abroad, no matter how settled and involved you are, Ireland retains a pull on your heartstrings, and you search out people and ways to ward off the homesickness. I put a lot of work into the class, brought in Irish music for us to listen to, always started with a prayer in Irish, and ended with social time for chat and Irish goodies. We always ended the semester with a party; traditional Irish dancing and fun. Jennifer always came to these and she learned to dance the reel and jig with the best of them. All of my siblings, living nearby or just visiting, were also part of these gatherings. I loved the dancing, and knowing my brother was the best waltz partner, always grabbed him or booked him in advance.

From the classes, other interests and outlets developed; I would meet someone for lunch and a book exchange of Irish authors. We swapped recipes, especially at Christmas, the sheer joy of an original Irish Christmas Cake, in the U. S. of A., used to blow my mind! It was like being part of a network; all the same, struggling in the same way and needing the familiarity of each other. No matter that we were here by choice, as in ready to be away from Ireland and the confines we felt, we greeted each other every time like family.

We located, and made everyone else aware of, the best import stores. I remember the first time I walked into one, I thought I had died and gone to Heaven. Who knew the sight of a tin of Batchelor's beans, or a bag of Odlum's flour, could send one into ecstasy!! And we hadn't even caught sight of the Kimberley biscuits or the Cadbury's bars yet. There was also a ready supply of CDs and Books, so these places were well worth a visit.

My First Christmas away from Ireland was made tolerable by the food supply stocked by these stores, especially for the holiday. We all used to scoff at everyone back home, so confident of their Christmas crackers and Selection boxes, and having no idea of the energy and phone calls of store locations and stock that went into securing them here. Of course, it had little to do with the actual items, and more to do with the fact that everything was, for us, a tie to home and the familiar; the memories associated from past years with our own families back home. My first Christmas here, I flew to my sister up North, it was the best idea; my brother had returned to Ireland until after the New Year, and I was in search of an Irish Christmas, and hers was the closest to it that I could get. I enjoyed the time to catch up with her and to get reacquainted with my nephew, but I knew that for any future Christmas, I would create my own and include family and friends, and any Irish ex pats who had nowhere else to go. I don't think my sister realized, but she was spending an American Christmas, with her husband's American relatives, and there was nothing familiar or familial about the experience for me. I wanted the opportunity to bring back more of my grandmother's and my mother's traditions, and create a stronger link between the American and the Irish experience. I needed to incorporate the old and familiar, with the new.

Chapter Twenty-Four

Life continued, and, as time passed, I realized that I felt more at home here and that I truly belonged. There was no question of this being short term, and so I had freedom to delve more comfortably and fully into life here, because I knew it was permanent. I was also enjoying the substitute teaching, which I was offered about once a week. I taught kids from Kindergarten all the way up. In the beginning, it reminded me of the classes I had in Ireland.

I loved being in the classroom, and not a day went by that I wasn't asked all about home and how the education experiences compared. I was highly amused when I was asked to teach religion to all the grades, knowing that it was purely because I came from Catholic Ireland. I loved it though, and it was still early enough into my time here, that I could really enjoy the kids' accent, almost as much as they enjoyed mine. Everyone commenting on the brogue was highly entertaining for me; especially as I myself couldn't hear it!!

I continued happy with Jennifer and her Dad, and life was now punctuated by newly established traditions, and Jennifer's progress through school, and her occasional bouts of ill health. Looking at her, you would never know that she had a serious health issue. I could go a little further and say, even living with her, you wouldn't have guessed. She needed therapy three times a day and was on a medication regime. She needed a healthy diet of lots of good nutritious food, but other than that, she was like every other kid. Thanks to her Dad her life was kept like this. So, on the intermittent occasions when she came down with a cold and developed a bronchial infection, it was always a shock to see how quickly her health could deteriorate.

While we lived a very normal life, and Jennifer's restrictions were few, there was an awareness of the importance of a consistent level of care, without making her feel smothered or burdened. I remember once when her Dad was away, I had heard her coughing in the night and it seemed more than usual. I kept her home the following day and took her for a checkup. Over cautious perhaps, but I knew instinctively that this is what her Dad would want me to do while she was in my care. She would recover from these bouts and take up her life with renewed energy.

The relationship for both of us changed many times; we were friends, sisters, mother /daughter, all rolled up in one. As she entered her teens, our most fun times, apart from hours spent lying on her bed gossiping, were spent shopping. She had her own particular style and she loved to go to the various malls around, especially as her biggest complaint of her Dad at that time was, "my Dad thinks the only place to buy anything is Sears".

Chapter Twenty-Five

Ihad been living at 91 for about eighteen months, when one night, my sister and some friends, came by to drag me to a new club. That scene was so not a part of my social life, but I went along, honestly because I thought they needed a designated driver. I didn't even bother to change and told them I was available only to 1am, take it or leave it. They were happy with this plan, so off we went. The club was only fifteen minutes away, and when we arrived the parking lot was packed. It was easy enough to get in though, and we found a table quickly, once we got inside.

It was a nice place; soft lights and no too loud music and they served food as well as drinks. I remember settling in for a couple of hours of chat and fun. Each table had a phone with its own number, clearly displayed, making it possible to dial any other table in the club and chat to whomever. This seemingly was the whole appeal of the place; you could talk on the phone and see the person at the same time. Cell phones in every hand hadn't arrived yet.

There was only one guy that I was aware of. I had seen him looking at our table. He had black hair and brown eyes and I thought he was really cute. He sent the waiter over to say drinks were on him, and then he dialed the table; he

wanted to speak to me!! When I first heard his voice, I felt
weak! He was Armenian and spoke with accented English;
it sounded so appealing and sexy.

I had gone out with a couple of guys before, whom I had
met through the Irish social network, but I had never felt
like this, or ever met anyone like him. We talked for a few
minutes, and then we danced and danced and talked and
talked, and when it was time to leave we went outside and
made plans to go into the city. My friends and his friends
too, all decided to go for a meal in New York. In my head,
I'm thinking, what are you doing? You don't know this guy,
he could be anyone! Crazy!! I couldn't help myself; I went
along for dinner at 3am, followed by a walk along the streets
of New York.

What can I say? Sidewalks never looked so good! I wanted
to walk all night. As we talked, I heard echoes of myself; he
too was trying to free himself from the constraints of too
much family, trying to find his own niche. Afterwards, I
went home and slept for a few hours, woke up, then thought,
did I switch planets in the last twelve hours? I had called
my sister up north before I went to bed and told her I had
met the guy I was going to marry. Only that she knew I
never had a drink, she might have thought I was drunk! Or
crazy! We met again the following day, and as soon as I saw
him, I knew, again and with certainty; this is my beloved,
my future husband. I had fallen in love! Another divine
intervention!! Thank you God!

It was March 1989, and my first St. Patrick's Day with
him was six days after we met. We celebrated in true Irish
style and both still remember it vividly today. This was his
first time to listen to the endless repertoire of Irish music, to
eat the traditional foods and to see the spontaneous nature

of the Irish themselves. We sang and danced, and ate the Irish food brought in especially for March 17th, and at the end of the night he was already looking forward to next year. He gave me a framed Newspaper article about the day, and I still have it.

For the Irish in Ireland, and England, and any other country, who have not celebrated this day here, all I can say is, you can hardly imagine it. The American love of all things Irish comes out on display everywhere you look, and it is movement and music, and love of all that is green! to the power of one million. You think you can imagine it, but really, you have to see it to believe it!

Chapter Twenty-Six

For the next year, we were inseparable. Midweek, we explored the local restaurants and sat into the early hours talking. Every weekend, we went somewhere. We discovered the State parks nearby, and he availed of the chance to show off his barbecuing skills. Such mundane tasks as shopping in a grocery store, for steak or lamb, became a romantic moment! And who knew your first taste of a green pepper and tomato, cooked by the love of your life, could send your taste buds into over-drive!

We drove around the countryside, holding hands, and marveled at the Universe, and our being together. In the summer we spent every weekend at the beach, getting bronzed together and not having a care in the world. We would saunter off the beach, and find a restaurant for dinner and talk into the early hours. We discovered that we were both searching for a life to value, and got little glimpses of what that would look like.

Life was good and we enjoyed ourselves. He was a jeweler by profession and worked late some weekends; on those Fridays I would drive to meet him and we would socialize with his friends. There was a ship, docked not too far from the George Washington Bridge that had been turned into a restaurant/bar, and this became our favorite place to hang out. Together, we celebrated birthdays and promotions, and romantic anniversaries, and over time we became a couple.

Unlikely perhaps, Irish and Armenian, but we both knew our cultures were more similar than not. Both cultures were based on a strong Christian value system, and revered the family unit. He had been born in Istanbul and educated in Heidelberg, Germany, and the inability to be free to be Christian, in a predominantly Muslim country, was among the motivators to leave and start life over in the U.S. He had come to the States initially by himself, and stayed with an aunt and uncle. He easily found work as a specialized Diamond setter, in the Diamond district in New York.

It was a time, for him, of freedom from obligations, and he had fun. A twenty-something, in New York City, with everything you can imagine at your fingertips. He made friends and enjoyed his work and soon knew he was here to stay. He began to save and think about his family joining him. He found an apartment and got it ready to accommodate a family. It was two years after his own arrival that his Mother and younger brother arrived. He had another brother, who would also join the family, but was delayed a further year, due to visa issues. His father decided not to come here, so for the next few years, my not yet husband! found himself in the role of provider for his Mother and brothers.

When he talks about it now, I can see that while it was the expected route to go, especially in his culture, he felt a certain sense of being robbed of his freedom. He also felt that he was being asked to be responsible before his time. How many twenty-two year olds today would take on the role and that level of responsibility? However, he managed, and he knew that some day in his future he would have a family of his own. When I hear him say this, of course it sounds like an affirmation of my own search.

When I met him, his immediate family consisted of his mother and two brothers; the youngest Alex was only thirteen. I didn't meet any of his family until we had been seeing each other for over a year and were ready to announce our engagement. In the Armenian culture, a son only brings the woman he intends to marry, never a casual girlfriend, to meet his family. Once you are introduced, you are welcomed with open arms, and immediately treated as a daughter.

I remember well the dinner that was arranged, for me to meet everyone. I thought my family was big! That night I think I met every Armenian in the State. It was a little overwhelming, but the food was delicious and the welcome was immense. After that, I went there frequently, was included in all the family gatherings and gradually we all got to know each other. Initially the language was a barrier, but as I learned Turkish and they learned English, we soon resolved this and mixed language conversation became the norm.

Many evenings when he was tied up at work, I would drive to his Mom's, eat dinner and hang out until he arrived home himself. His younger brother Alex was always home and we watched TV and became competitive about the answers on Jeopardy and Wheel of Fortune. We chatted and he became my kid brother too. We spent many Saturday nights having dinner with each of the aunts and uncles. It was a great way for me to get to know them and be spoiled with the traditional food, which I was quickly coming to love. We ate lamb and shish kebabs, Kufta and shepherd's salad. I remember one night, during one of the many backyard feasts and barbecues we stayed there singing and chatting until three in the morning. I remember thinking to myself that the language and the food may be a little different, but we could have been an Irish gathering.

I soon got into the habit of visiting the various family members by myself and it was enjoyable; a way to learn more about my husband to be, without his being there. I was invited to all the Bridal showers and Baby showers, and felt comfortable up to a point. I knew my discomfort had nothing to do with the actual people and more to do with echoing reminders of being uncomfortable in a similar setting.

This would follow me always, and I could only forgive myself and not resort to self injury, by reminding myself of how far I had already come. Sometimes this was enough, but other times it was not. So even if on the outside, I looked fine, and that I was getting on with life, the old issues continued to crop up in my mind; I struggled and it was sometimes very hard. I luckily had the luxury of some of my own family nearby and this helped.

You can get comfort from being able to say to your sibling, I don't think I can stay here, and there are no questions, and you have company as you go outside to recover. By this time, I not only had a brother here, but two other sisters had also settled in this State. They received the same welcome, and enjoyed the Armenian hospitality as much as I. Many evenings, before a night out, we would all arrive back to the house and his Mother would cook steaks and French fries for all of us. She welcomed us with the hospitality that my own country is famous for and I loved her for it.

Before we got engaged, I subjected my better half to an inspection by Jennifer and her Dad; if he made the grade with these two, we were home free. I remember setting up the table and cooking a special dinner, and I remember also, the look on Jennifer's Dad's face, as he viewed the preparations. All he said was, "Guess you really like this one, kid!", and of course, he was right. Jennifer pronounced him cute with a very sexy voice, and her Dad, while a little less vocal, gave the welcoming handshake with the words, "You're welcome to come back any time."

After he left the house that night, Jennifer and I sat up for hours indulging in girl talk and silliness. She was so funny; so excited and happy for me and wanted to know all our plans. She would ask questions I hadn't thought to ask myself, and we would take the conversation all over the place as we explored the possibilities. It was adorable and so great for me; I missed my own younger siblings especially, and she more than compensated. From that point on, she was in on everything and it became such a joy for me, at this special time, to have my live- in collaborator and co-conspirator!

We ended up having two Engagement parties. One was given by the Armenian side, and the other, by the Irish. All sides attended both events and it was such a unique and perfect idea. At the start of the Armenian bash, we had a short ceremony, when we prayed together and received plain gold bands to wear on the right hand, until our wedding. During the party, a representative from each family presented me, as the bride to be, with a piece of jewelry. In the culture, this is a tradition of honoring permanence and the value of the new member to all in the family. The celebration that night was an introduction of all my family and friends to the Armenian food and music. I was proud to be a part of all this love, and honored that so many of my new family were now friends. I was so appreciative of all the cousins, who, for the past year, had been willing interpreters, as I found my footing in this new Bi- lingual world. We ate and sang and danced until the early hours.

The following weekend, my brother hosted the Irish contingent, including students, now friends, from my Irish classes, and all the friends I had made since arriving in my adopted State. All of my future husband's family got to appreciate our food and music. We danced and sang and my funniest memory of the night is when my beloved asked if some of us were speaking in Irish. We were not, but we were speaking so fast, it sounded like it.

I remember afterwards, at 5am the next morning, giving thanks for the five hour time difference in Ireland and chatting on the phone with my mother. I remember the delirious feeling of happiness and excitement, for where the future might lead. She was thrilled for me and told me that all I ever wanted was a family of my own. It seemed like I had come full circle, and could now be free to just savor the moment and all the other moments, just waiting to be lived.

We planned to be married in October, of the year following our engagement, so plans were full steam ahead. Life, temporarily, had other ideas, and before that happened I had a health issue to take care of. I had been having some pain and thought it was my appendix. I went back to Dr. Silverman, who had helped with the mosquito allergies, and he diagnosed Gall Bladder Disease. I would need surgery to have it removed. He referred me to a surgeon and I set up an appointment.

All through this process, I was very conscious of my scars from the self inflicted injuries. I had no idea how I would explain them, if asked. It was coming into summer and I couldn't wear long sleeves. I finally plucked up the courage to mention it to Dr. Silverman, emphatically explaining this was past tense. He was so kind and understanding; he had a chat with the surgeon and the issue never came up after that. I remember thinking at the time, that this was another opportunity to recognize the old life as in the past, and the new one as separate. I think that this, more than anything, allowed me to move forward and be comfortable with myself. All I could think was Thank you God, another miracle for you, and another sigh of relief for me.

The surgery was set for July '91, and I would need a week to recover. My sister agreed to come and stay with Jennifer, and my future mother-in-law offered to have me stay with her; she would take care of me as I got well. The surgery went smoothly, I believe I rambled and then some as I came out of anesthesia. Jennifer came to see me with her Dad, one of my first visitors, and she teased me for weeks afterwards about not making any sense. I remember I was in a sort of pressure bubble to prevent a blood clot. It felt weird, but I was glad of the precaution. Later, Dr. Silverman dropped in to see me, and told me my surgeon was a heart guy; I was lucky to be getting such preventative care. Little did he know how prophetic these words were; in the very near future I would go to the hospital twice to have a blood clot dissolved. I felt great, and was feeling so much better that I was ready to be out of the hospital. I stayed one night and was then discharged, to spend a week with my soon to be in laws.

It was the perfect place to be. So quiet and peaceful and for the first couple of days all I did was sleep. I remember being on pain killers, and by day two, wishing I didn't feel so bad. I was all weepy and miserable, talking to my mother in Ireland, asking her when and if I would ever feel normal. She was crying too and I felt so comforted. She had

had the same surgery many years prior and she said to be patient and you will feel good in about a week. I will forever appreciate the generosity of being taken care of that week. I ate delicious hot food, had help getting up, and help settling into a chair so I could watch T.V. In this tender caring place, I recovered, and on the last day, we all went out to a Turkish restaurant to celebrate. The only good by product of all this, is that I lost a lot of weight, and could visualize the skinny me in a killer wedding gown! Amazing how shallow we can be in the midst of such profound experience!

Chapter Twenty-Seven

My parents had shared many conversations by phone, with both of us, and my father had received THE call, to request his daughter's hand in marriage. They were eagerly looking forward to coming for the event, and meeting their soon to be son-in-law. I imagine they were anxious to see me also; it had been a while and phone calls and letters are no substitute for being face to face. Most of my siblings and my best friend from school had also marked the date.

Anyone who has planned a wedding knows what a project it can be. We looked at invitation samples, reception venues, menus, party favors. We chose bridesmaid colors and tuxedo styles. We booked a Limo, a photographer and a videographer. We compiled a guest list, revised it and then revised it again. We met and overcame all the obstacles that are inevitable for all weddings. My mother agreed to do the wedding cake and it would be in the traditional Irish style. Jennifer and her Dad were my personal supporters through this time, Jennifer especially. She came with me and my sisters when we shopped for the wedding gown, and was vocal about what looked good and not! It was fabulous fun and I enjoyed every second. She helped to choose shoes and an evening bag, and advised on hair styles; and I enjoyed an evening with her as we both tried out styles. She was to be a bridesmaid and was beside herself with excitement.

I was thrilled that my wedding would also be a family reunion of sorts. I had left Ireland in June '87 and was getting married on October 20, 1991, so it was almost four and a half years since I had seen my parents and some siblings. It was probably the longest we had been apart. I had some reservations and worried about their involvement in this, my new life. But I need not have worried, they so appreciated being there, and I was so wrapped up in the momentum of the upcoming event, that talking through anything serious was not on the agenda. I knew that at some point in the future we would have a conversation, but not yet, not this visit.

A couple of months before the wedding, we decided that we would look for an apartment in the town where I was living, and got lucky in finding one about ten minutes drive from Jennifer and her Dad. It was in an old Victorian house, over one hundred years old, quaint and with an obvious sense of history. We had the apartment to the front of the house, and had the bonus of a wrap around deck. We were both outdoor space lovers and this is what cinched the deal. It was the perfect starting place for us, and it had enough room for a guest if anyone wanted to stay. It was so much fun setting up our first home. Love certainly gets put to the test when you go searching for home furnishings together! We were not too different from each other in terms of taste, luckily, and found what we needed, and had the apartment set up before the big day.

We also had to attend a pre marriage course, required by both Armenian and Catholic churches. The one we enrolled

in had a class once a week, for six weeks. They covered all
practical issues that go hand in hand with joining two lives. I
wouldn't say we enjoyed it, we endured it. It ended with each
couple being interviewed by the priest. The only memorable
moment for me, of the entire course, was when my future
husband was asked about his ideas re children. His response
was, that if God gave us a child, he hoped we would feel
blessed and do the best possible for that child. I just found
it touching that he could be so vulnerable and honest. It
also confirmed for me, that we were both of the same mind
and heart, in relation to the core issues. The months passed,
everyday life being lived alongside all the planning. And
like every special day, it started off being months away, then
weeks, and then it arrived and we were ready.

Finally, it was October 10th, and my parents and my
youngest sister, who is also my God-daughter, arrived from
Ireland. It was so fabulous to have them here, and that first
night we went to dinner and they met my beloved and
of course could immediately see why I loved him. They
couldn't stop saying how happy they were for me. I had the
uncanny feeling that they were guests in my life, and this
allowed me to stay emotionally separated from them, to the
extent that I needed to be. They met Jennifer and her Dad,
and actually stayed at the house for the festivities.

At the time I thought this was too close for comfort
and was not exactly thrilled, but it was fine. A week of
whirlwind activity followed, and every day we did something
in preparation for the wedding. The five tier wedding cake
my mother had made arrived in her suitcase, and she spent
a day putting the marzipan on, and another day doing the
final icing. It was so special for me to have that cake, and
we took it in the car to the reception venue with the care

it deserved. It was a work of art when it was assembled. It represented another Irish tradition transplanted to my new American life.

Meanwhile, my other siblings arrived, and my friend of twenty years also. Everything and everyone was in place for the big day. We devoted another evening to dinner with the two sets of parents, along with other family members. That dinner was something else. We communicated mostly by facial expression and gestures. They spoke Turkish to each other, naturally, and just because we could, we all spoke Irish. My sisters and I really enjoyed seeing my parents in this strange environment, but they handled it pretty well. It was hilarious. We were all loud but the general understanding was that we were all having a great time. It was a nice way to break the ice and now we felt they could at least nod at each other, with some level of recognition, for our big day.

Chapter Twenty-Eight

On the morning of October 20th, my soon to be husband sent a vase of red roses; such a lovely surprise and such a perfect way to start our day. All during the morning friends and neighbors dropped by, wishing us well and wanting to see the bride. My parents were fascinated by all these friends, and it gave them a glimpse of the life I had created, since leaving Ireland. My father would shake his head in wonderment, saying, "It's great to see you so happy". The Wedding ceremony was at 3pm, so we had plenty of time for hair and makeup, followed by chat and laughter, and giggles and trips down memory lane.

My mother helped me to get ready, settled the veil she had made for me, and then stood back to tell me how beautiful I looked. I am so thankful for this time with her; she was so in awe of my beautiful gown and the choice of dresses for the bridesmaids. She walked with me down the stairs and watched with me, the look of pride on my father's face, as he stood at the bottom. On some level, they both knew what I had been through, even though we had never talked about any of it in a really honest way. This was a day of celebration, and I knew in my heart that I had made the right choice for myself, to move from Ireland. I gave thanks that they could both be there to share my day; despite all the previous difficulties, I wanted, and was thankful for, my parents' presence. Any further search for connection would wait for another time.

Jennifer had persuaded her Dad to allow her to wear makeup, and she couldn't wait to get her face on. She looked so beautiful and grown up. We took plenty of photos when we were all ready to leave for the church. All my bridesmaids; four of my sisters and Jennifer, were in black and white, carrying matching fans and purses, they looked so elegant. I got a call that the groom was running late, so should wait until I knew he was at the church. He arrived at 3.30 and has never been allowed to forget it!! The ceremony was a traditional Catholic Mass, concelebrated by the priest of my parish, the Armenian pastor from my husband's church and my Jesuit priest/ student of my Irish classes, who was there as a special surprise.

My father walked me down the aisle with tears in his eyes. Despite all the pain in our history I knew that both he and my mother were happy, glad they could travel to be with me for my special day. It was a beautiful ceremony; my youngest sister (who is also my Goddaughter) sang all the hymns, and both my father and Jennifer's did the readings. Friends and other family members did the Prayers of the Faithful, my nephew carried the rings and he was accompanied by my husband's cousin. Both of our mothers brought up the gifts at the offertory. When it came time for the sharing of the sign of peace, I walked down to my family and friends gathered, and hugged all my brothers and sisters and my parents, and of course, Jennifer. My husband followed suit with his family.

This was an event to join more than one man and one woman; it would be the event that would allow me to put the past pain more fully behind me and I would have a new and different relationship with my parents. I was a grown woman, joined to a husband who loved her, who dearly wished for children of their own, and who both knew that there was nothing ordinary about the way they had met or the love they felt for each other. After it was over, I floated down the aisle on the arm of my new husband, beaming at the congregation; we were officially Mr. and Mrs.

The reception followed, and we were all announced and proudly took our places for the first dance, my bridesmaids and their partners joining us. My brother serenaded us with, "you've got a friend", telegrams from absent family in Ireland were read, and then we sat to catch our breath. My father welcomed my husband into the family, and told him he had gotten himself a diamond and precious gem! I gave a speech that united all the different people in my life, and spoke in three languages so everyone was included. It was part Irish, English and Turkish. I felt so blessed and grateful. Apart from my family from Ireland, we had relatives from Turkey also, and from other States around the U.S.

While I was thrilled they could all be there, I used my speech to especially thank my youngest brother, Fintan. He had arrived just the day before and I remember telling him how it made my day to have him present. I also honored Jennifer, foregoing the usual throwing of the bouquet, and presenting it to her instead. It was a total surprise, and so much fun, to have her accept it from me. I wanted her to know how I valued our relationship, and that, to me, she was truly special.

We danced to Turkish music first, and these traditional

dances are something to behold. All fluid movement in time to the music, and after the first two, all the Irish crowd were on the dance floor. You don't necessarily need a partner as there are so many dance styles going on at the same time, you just join in. My brothers escorted Armenian girls on the dance floor and it was truly a blending of the cultures.

And then the beat changed; friends of ours had brought an Irish CD and the tempo suddenly jumped. Sparks flew and the atmosphere was charged. The Irish crowd were tapping their feet in time to the music and chomping at the bit to grab a partner and get out there. We did reels and waltzes, and lined up for the siege of Ennis and swapped partners as we circled the dance floor. We screamed and roared and generally got a little carried away. I waltzed with my father and I remember there were times when my feet barely touched the floor! I stood beside Fintan as we all danced in a circle and watched his curls shake in time to the music. I grabbed my older brother for a waltz because I wanted the thrill of being danced off my feet. Jennifer and her Dad got so into it that I can see her reluctant to stop, hanging onto her dad's arm, as she tries to catch her breath. These are more than memories; they are treasured pictures still in my head of such a special day, not just our getting married, but that we had all these family and friends with us to bring it all together. Who knew? I surely didn't; only a little over four years earlier, as I left Ireland, that this was even a possibility. It goes back to being open to whatever the Universe and Divine providence send your way.

It was sad to see the evening end, but we all agreed that it had been memorable and so enjoyable for all. Our limo drove us to our new apartment, and we would leave for the Poconos the next day. We both wanted a few days, just us; with all the entertaining of the relatives and the wedding preparation of the previous weeks, we were ready to be alone. We chose the perfect time of year to get married. I remember walking, arm in arm, through the trails around the hotel, and hearing our feet crunch in the newly fallen leaves.

We visited farm stalls along quiet country roads and savored the feeling of being away from the hustle and bustle. We discovered quaint tiny restaurants and enjoyed clam chowder. Our suite was fun and fabulous; we had our own swimming pool and Jacuzzi, separated by a glass wall, and a cozy living room with a fireplace, which we used every evening. And the hotel dining room was a short walk away. We just loved being together and making plans. We both felt like we were starting a wonderful journey, and we couldn't wait to see where it took us.

We returned home to our own apartment, and such bliss to finally have a place just to ourselves. My family would be returning to Ireland soon, so we planned a big family dinner together at the apartment. We both like to cook, so it was a mix of Irish /Armenian fare. I had such mixed feelings; here were my worlds joined, and it was all so smooth and perfect, and we all had had such a good time, and now I had to say Goodbye! It was very hard, I would miss seeing my youngest sister especially, but I knew she would return for a visit.

My mother had been so much a part of my wedding day and I felt such appreciation for her, and my father had been there to walk me down the aisle. We were at a different place, perhaps better to say I was in a different place, and they were able to join me. I felt for the first time the possibility of a relationship that wasn't based on my being a vulnerable child subject to parental control.

I guess I had grown up, and forgiven them, for the emptiness in my young life, and had found understanding for them at the same time as I had found love, with my husband. It would take time though, for me to be able to put the judgmental feelings behind me, but for now, I was happy and could wait for the future conversation that I knew needed to take place. They returned to Ireland early November and married life for us began.

Chapter Twenty-Nine

My husband continued to work in the Jewelry business and I continued to care for Jennifer. Jennifer and I had made a fun pact before I got married. If her Dad drove her nuts, she would come and stay with us, and if my husband drove me crazy, I would come and stay with her. This silliness allowed us to keep our connection. She was so happy for me and we continued to enjoy our already established routine. My husband and I entertained on the weekends, it was our turn to have family and friends come to us, now that we had some space. I loved having Jennifer and her Dad over, it was a chance to return all the hospitality shown to my family and friends at '91'.

At this time, I had two sisters living nearby, my brother, who had been so welcoming to me on my arrival here, had decided to return to Ireland; the computer firm he worked for were opening a branch in Dublin and the opportunity to return to the Homeland was too good to miss. My brother Fintan, having decided to chase his own American dream, was living and working close to us also.

Our first Christmas, only months after getting married, we decided to host all the members of our immediate families. We joined the best of our traditions, and it was the first Christmas that I had no nostalgia for home. I was at home, and the twinges of home sickness were gone. We walked to the Midnight service, it was a chilly night with snow in the forecast, and we had plenty of time to walk. I can still hear the choir, the familiar carols bringing the season to life. We looked out the windows and saw the snow falling. Could we have asked for a more perfect setting, as we spent our first holiday together? After the service, we walked home holding hands, and stopped along the way to kiss, shout Merry Christmas, and give thanks for the blessings and having found each other. I remember asking the Universe to keep us safe with each other and for both of us to never take what we had for granted.

Christmas morning dawned bright and clear and so our car driving guests would be safe in travelling. Our apartment looked gloriously festive. The tree, proudly displaying its mix of cultural decorations, had pride of place in the living room, and our mantle with the first of my growing collection of Mr. and Mrs. Claus, displayed all the Christmas cards from family, both here and abroad. The table was traditional with our centerpiece of holly and berries, and at each place setting we had the Irish Crackers. The guests would open these as they sat down, and then don their paper hats. For me, and my siblings, this was a wonderful gathering; acknowledging our memories of Christmas growing up.

Everything I had seen my Grandmother and Mother do, I did. I would always try to have them there by being like them and remembering how they had done things. If somebody said this is just like home, I felt the women before me were honored. My mother-in-law and the other members of my new family were amazed and awed and delighted to be included. My husband's grandmother joined us that Christmas; she had recently come to live with the family in the U.S.

We didn't know it then, but this would be the only Christmas that we would celebrate, all together. I remember my husband ruffling his Grandmother's hair and pulling crackers with her, and later snuggling up to her for a picture. The only chance he would have to create such a memory. We exchanged gifts, and overate, and later sang carols as we drank Turkish coffee and Irish tea, and the celebration ended as we cut our inevitable Christmas cake. We waved them all off as the evening turned dark, and were delighted with ourselves, as we had set the bar for many Christmases to come.

Chapter Thirty

The next year, 1992, was for the most part, unremarkable, except for the special party we threw for my baby brother-in-law, Alex, as he turned sixteen. The apartment had a huge wrap around deck and this is where we set up the tables, and we were able to host thirty people. My husband manned the barbecue and all the family brought special dishes. My mother-in-law outdid herself with her kufta and burek, stuffed peppers and tomatoes. I baked the cake and lovingly included his favorite whipped cream and fresh fruit as part of the dessert. Alex was so proud that night and so appreciative; he thanked both of us for doing this for him.

Alex looked up to my husband, as a father figure; their father being absent, and my husband being the older brother by fifteen years. Alex especially loved that the party was a surprise; we didn't do it on the exact day, and he thought he was just coming to dinner. We talked and sang, little knowing that at the young age of thirty-two, he would pass away; unexpectedly and tragically, leaving a huge sense of loss.

My husband and I continued to enjoy each other and married life and included family and friends for all our celebrations. Ours was the gathering house; the place to come together. On many a Saturday night, we would be about to throw a couple of steaks on the grill and the doorbell would ring, and it's a case of grab a few more steaks, add some chairs, and voila! we are having another party.

The next to celebrate a special birthday was my youngest brother Fintan, who turned twenty-one in January of 1993. It was a celebration very close to my heart, as we had become close to him since he had decided to remain in the States. He lived only minutes from us and we would see him a couple of times a week. He was welcome for dinner any night and he often came by, ate, and then left to do his own thing. Sometimes, he would hang out and crash in our spare room. While he was working he was fine, but he got to a place where he wasn't working enough and he began to sink into depression. A week would pass, and if I hadn't seen him, I would drop over and if he didn't answer I would just leave a bag of food at the door. I knew he would come over when he was ready. It was a very difficult time for him and I worried

One night, he was staying with us, and I went to check if he needed anything and he was sitting on the bed with my kitchen carving knife in his hand. I think my heart might have stopped. He was having difficulties similar to my own earlier experience, and it broke my heart to see such pain. I took him to my friend, Dr. Silverman, and he talked with him for a while and then referred him to a psychiatrist. Unfortunately, this doctor was not a good match for Fintan, and it would take a future return to Ireland for him to find a professional with whom he was comfortable working. I remember thinking, as his birthday approached, I wanted him to know how loved and cherished he was, and so we pulled out all the stops for the 21st.

We invited his friends to join family members, as we made plans to celebrate the event. As per tradition it was a barbecue, and this time the cake was a joint effort by me and my two sisters and when we put it in front of him he said, "This cake looks just like one the mother would make". It was the ultimate compliment. We had a wonderful night. Over the next couple of years, Fintan would move in with a brother or sister and continue to work and seem happy, but would battle his demons on a regular basis. He would return to Ireland in the late '90s. I was so glad to have had the chance to do this for him, for sadly, again tragedy awaited us; Fintan would pass away at age thirty-one, the first major shared loss for me and my siblings.

Chapter Thirty-One

Early in 1994, just before Valentine's Day, my husband and I started to rethink a many times previously discussed idea; that we should think about a move to another part of the United States. My husband was anxious to start a business of his own, and knew that proximity to New York was a disadvantage to the type of business he had in mind. He had a vision of a show room where customers could feel welcome in a more intimate setting, with an equipped workshop where he could design and make custom pieces of jewelry.

I shared and supported his dream, but at that time, all I could think about, and dream about, was a quieter town that would support our wish for family life. I had suffered through two miscarriages; one early term, and one at the advanced stage of eighteen weeks. Both of these losses devastated both of us. We were puzzled and confused and there had been no conclusive medical reason for either loss. We had simply been told to try and stay positive. The only constructive suggestion was from my friend, the general practitioner, Dr. Silverman, who thought that perhaps a less stressful and less busy work life might be what we needed.

We both knew, I think, that where we were living was not

where we wanted to live for the foreseeable future; certainly not where we could see ourselves raising a child. In fact, we had talked about possible options, on and off for about a year. Neither of us was tied to a work situation, it was as if we had been waiting for this. Jennifer was now old enough to be on her own and I was no longer involved in her day to day care. We still saw each other and had long chats on the phone. She came to our apartment for sleepovers and also when her dad was out of town. We shopped together frequently, and I was always involved in her birthdays and Christmas. I continued to get my Irish fix with her dad, with visits and phone chats. He was, and always will be for me, the epitome of what is home and Ireland; possibly because he was the one to offer me the perfect home when I first arrived, and also because he has always celebrated and enjoyed all that is Irish, our shared heritage. I knew that even if we no longer lived close by we would always stay in touch. My husband had been working independently in New York, and so, had only to pack up his tools and find a sublet for the space, and he was ready to go.

It was no great surprise, when after some more discussion, we decided, now or never. We had no major commitments; we were renting the apartment and we could be moved as early as next month. And that's exactly what we did. We got out a map and looked around; we knew we wanted to go South, but beyond that, had really no clear idea. We decided on Georgia, and we also agreed that my husband would go first, pick somewhere randomly within the State and then we would see.

To anyone else this might seem totally insane, but remember we had left our own countries and come here to the States with practically nothing, so really, what did we have to lose? I will admit we both had a very well developed faith in Divine Providence and believed we had been guided so well up to now.

He left with a single suitcase and not a lot of money. We were both devastated by the idea of being away from each other, but we both knew in our hearts that this is what we had to do. I stayed and got busy. I held a huge yard sale, with my sisters and Jennifer helping, sold everything we knew was not necessary, and ended up with enough to finance the move. My husband called; the train he was on had stopped in Virginia, there were some electrical issues and no more trains were running that night. He found a hotel and got chatting during dinner to a local businessman. His story was told, as stories get told in these situations, and before he went to sleep he knew his trip the next day would include a slight detour. We would not be going any further south; he had found our small town.

Initially, we knew he would get a job in a jewelry store, as we were in no position to finance a business just yet. On the advice of the stranger at dinner the previous night, he knew of a couple of stores in this town, who might be interested in his skills. He decided to drop in, introduce himself and see if there was a vacancy. He had a nice conversation, offered to work the next day to show his skills, and by the next evening, he had a job. He called me immediately and we both screamed down the phone lines!! Now I could come for a visit and see my future home, and spend a few days exploring accommodation. The bonus was to see my husband. I was so excited I could hardly sleep.

I set off with my sister and we drove until we arrived into Virginia, passing green fields and Horse farms and dairies along the way, and both of us said at the same time, "remind you of Ireland, wouldn't it", and we couldn't wait to get to the small town. My husband had forgotten that my mental image for the words, 'small town,' had its origin in Ireland; where it means a main street with a shop, a church, a post office and a school. This was not a small town!

I remember calling Jennifer and her Dad to let them know I had arrived. I knew they could clearly hear the disappointment in my voice, but I recovered and agreed to give the place a chance. My husband was still in a hotel at this point, and our main goal that weekend was to find an apartment. I had arrived Saturday afternoon, and we went to dinner that night, to talk about what we should do next.

Chapter Thirty-Two

We drove around, and I was willing to admit the place had possibilities. So we got a map and a real estate booklet with apartments for rent. We got up on Sunday and off we went, from one complex to another, in search of our home. Some were horrific; too many people in one place for me and I felt totally overcome with claustrophobia. I knew I couldn't live in a place without immediate access to the outdoors; it had to have a deck or a patio.

We looked at about ten apartments that day and by 4.30 that afternoon we still had nothing. Finally, we pulled into the last one on the list. There were vacancies, it was only two stories high, all had a balcony and I remember thinking, "Alleluia!" We took it immediately, it was March 22nd and I would arrive down in exactly one week, having arranged for the furniture to be moved. We were thrilled because we were out of time. I was going back to the Garden State the next day and my husband had a new job to go to.

It was an insane week, but it was easier to live through it knowing that I was going to be rejoining my husband again and we could support each other, by being there, instead of just on the phone. The moving van came and picked up all the furniture and boxes, my sisters and my husband's family helped me pack. It was my last day suddenly and now time for another round of goodbyes. I knew I would see my own family very soon, as they would come and visit.

I drove over to say goodbye to Jennifer and her Dad, not knowing when I would see them again; I was after all moving four hundred miles south. Not exactly a trip to take and meet someone for dinner, it would require planning and time. I knew it would be a while before I would see them again. I can still see Jennifer standing and waving on the steps, as I drove away. I was ready to head south that afternoon, to rejoin my husband and begin the new life that awaited us.

I next went and had the car checked out, filled it with gas, and then hit the highway. It was 3pm and I hoped to see my husband by 11pm, at the latest. I was not thrilled to be going solo on such a long car ride, but I thought "To heck with it", I am not waiting any longer. The trip was fine, except for one mishap; I had a tire blow out just after passing DC. I pulled the car across the lanes of the highway and Thank God came to a safe stop. Thankfully, some other driver called the cops and within ten minutes there was a patrol car pulling up behind me.

I was never so happy to see a police cruiser in my life. He called a tow truck; I had to wait about an hour but they replaced my tire, and then I was on my way again. I pulled into the hotel parking lot three hours later than I had intended, at 3am, but it was joyous. I saw my husband standing there, and I said to myself, "OK, I am here; now it's all fine". We stayed at the hotel for a couple of nights, it was March 29th 1994, and we would get the keys to our new apartment on April 1st.

We sat waiting, three days later, for the moving truck to arrive. We had a cooler to sit on and we had eaten dinner on paper plates. I couldn't wait to be reunited with all our stuff. With all the crazy stories one hears of peoples' stuff going missing; I wouldn't relax until I saw it. We only had to wait a short time, the truck arrived, and then we were opening doors and giving directions where everything needed to go. We spent the rest of that night settling in and rearranging our furniture. We were happy to be here in the new location, excited to be back together, and ready to start this new chapter in our lives.

Chapter Thirty-Three

The following day, I dropped my husband to work, so I could have the car to explore. I drove everywhere and checked everywhere out; explored neighborhoods, located the post office, the dry cleaners and all the amenities I would need. I drove to the rural parts of town, in an effort to find something to connect with. I found the church and popped in to check it out. I found a bank and a movie theatre, and finally, was happy to say, "We have everything we need here". That evening we went grocery shopping together and then back to the apartment to cook. This was our routine for the next few months; adjusting to our new town. We were very happy with the simple life, as the important thing was just to be together.

For my husband, the longer he spent at his job, the more opportunities came his way to show the limitless scope of his talent. When I visited the store the owners would compliment his creative genius. I was glad he was happy and appreciated. I was getting familiar with our new location and beginning to meet new people and make friends. We had only been living there about four months when we discovered we were expecting our first child. I remember driving over to tell my husband, we were both ecstatic, and immediately we started to plan and imagine and dream!

I was fortunate once again, to find a kind and compassionate doctor, who, once he learned of my previous pregnancies, went out of his way with sonograms and testing to reassure me that this time we would have a baby. We told everyone, we couldn't wait. I remember calling both sets of parents and they were thrilled for us. My mother had lots of advice and I soaked it all up. I started to think of this baby as a person already, and somewhere within myself I knew it would be ok. Later that year, in October, we moved to a townhouse; we needed the extra space for a baby and I wanted a yard too.

My brothers came down from New Jersey to help us move, and we did it all in a few hours. I remember the four of us, sitting eating dinner that night and thinking, "Who would have known, Ireland to Virginia?" Both of my brothers remarked on the similarity to Ireland. We loved the new place and especially loved all the extra room. We celebrated Thanksgiving with local friends, and then immediately started to get excited for Christmas; I remember being especially thrilled because my older and wiser sister was coming for Christmas. It was such a special treat to have her here, I was five months pregnant and glowing, and I needed my family around me and she filled the gap for me.

I missed my mother especially at this time, and Ireland seemed farther away than before. My sister and I had a fun time together; buying small things for the baby and looking at all the baby furniture and strollers and toys. We continued our Christmas traditions and marveled at the idea of its being the last Christmas, just me and my husband. It was hard to believe and we prayed that next year, Please God! We would have our baby.

We rang in the New Year, 1995, with a special joy and anticipation. The baby was due on April 18th and it didn't seem that far away. My husband continued well in his job and he started to get special recognition for his own designs; showcased separately, away from the other merchandise. The store volume started to increase, as customers grew to know him, and want him to design for them. He was famous as the, 'one of a kind', guy. If you had an idea, he would get out his drawing pencils, and right before your eyes, your idea came to life. It was great to see him so fulfilled.

My own health continued well, and the baby and I were progressing nicely. The only thing I craved, apart from my mother's cooking, was Doritos, and my husband made many late night trips to the convenience store. One weekend in February we went shopping and got everything for the nursery in one trip.

The following weekend we set it all up, and from then on, every day, I used to stand in the doorway, just looking. I would find myself imagining what it would be like to walk in and see my baby sleeping, or walk in, first thing in the morning, and see the trusting eyes of my child looking back at me. I dreamed and dreamed and it was all good.

Chapter Thirty-Four

On the night of March 28th, I had a major craving for Chinese food, which was weird, as I had never eaten it before. My husband obliged and picked it up, and I ate more than he did. Afterwards, I took a shower and pampered myself, and lounged around reading a book. My husband had fallen asleep, and so shortly after midnight, I got up to creep quietly into bed and my water broke. I thought, "Oh! No, it's too early; this baby shouldn't be here for a couple of weeks yet". I called my Doctor, and he said, "I'm at the hospital already, I'll just stay here, when you feel it's too uncomfortable come on in and we'll take care of you."

I relaxed completely, knowing he was there. I let my husband continue sleeping while I packed a bag, then I took another shower, and gave myself a pedicure. All this time, I am talking to the baby, "It's OK, I know you want to arrive, just wait a little longer; we have a little more time before you get here". I remember being seriously impressed with myself; for being so calm!

As the time got close to 3am, I realized that I was waiting for it to be a civilized hour in Ireland, so that I could talk to my mother. I called and she picked up, and then I cried.

I told her what I had been doing. She said, "That's perfect, you will know when it's time to go to the hospital, and it's better to stay home as long as you think you can manage". Once I knew she knew what was going on, I relaxed again. We talked some more, my father picked up the extension, and they both wished me well and said they would be waiting to hear from us.

Shortly after this, I woke my husband up, and said, "It's time to go", and he said, "Go where?" I said, "The baby is coming, let's go to the hospital". We got there at 4.40am, got checked in, and the nurses asked if I wanted any medication. I said, "No thanks"; I felt high as a kite already with pure excitement and anticipation and if I got more drugged up, I might fly!! We didn't have to wait long as our Baby son arrived at 6.40am and it was indescribable. Utter wonder. "Thank you God!" was all I could say. This precious tiny being was ours, and relying totally on us for all his needs. I remember thinking I knew it was a boy all through my pregnancy and his name was always going to be Jonathan. There is enough joy in this moment of today to last me a lifetime.

The next thing I remember is being ravenous and devouring the entire contents of a breakfast tray in five minutes. Then I was ready to hit the phones. My first call was to Jennifer and her dad, and it was so delicious to hear Jennifer scream down the phone. I had already asked her, a month earlier, to be the baby's Godmother, and she had been beside herself with excitement, and so honored. I remember when I asked her she said, "Me? Are you sure? Oh my God, me a godmother, I'm so excited, what do I have to do, what will I wear for the baptism? I will be so good at it, I will be so cool," and on and on she went, her voice getting more high pitched as she talked, and then abruptly she said,

"Okay, we'll talk soon, I have to go and call my Dad." So it was natural for me to want to connect with that joy again, as soon as he was born, and as we talked that morning, she told me before she hung up that she was going to write a letter to my baby so that he would know her before she got to see him.

We called everyone else and told them our glorious news. I described him, "he's gorgeous", and the nurses smiled while telling me they loved my Irish accent. What accent? I still can't hear it!! Friends came by and brought flowers and balloons, and marveled at this new being. My husband and I slept together that night at the hospital, with the baby beside us, and I remember thinking, "does it get any better than this"?

The next morning, my Doctor came by and pronounced us both in great shape and ready to leave. Then the panic set in, we looked at each other and thought, are they crazy, we have no idea how to do this, but of course we reassured each other that we could figure it out.

Chapter Thirty-Five

We brought Jonathan home on a beautiful bright sunny morning, it was Thursday, and we would have help in two days when his paternal Grandma, his Yaya, would arrive on Saturday and help us with whatever we needed. I was so thrilled. If I couldn't have my own mother this was the next best thing. She came and looked after us, and let me look after my baby. I slept when the baby slept. I sat and held my baby, with the luxury of my mind free of everything else. She cooked for us and dinner was taken care of every night. I didn't even have to think of a menu. She went off shopping with my husband, and together they produced a gourmet meal every night and lots more for the freezer. I talked on the phone with my sisters and my mother. I chatted with Jennifer and kept her up to date. I talked to my brothers and all my extended family. Friends from Ireland started to call, as the news filtered out. I remember getting a call from the nuns, at the convent where I had gone to school in Ireland, and thinking, what a joy for them to be able to share in our special day. I talked to Fintan, to let him know his Godson had arrived, and he was delighted and promised to come see him in person soon.

About two weeks after Jonathan's arrival, it was Easter. We had a house full of bunnies and baby chicks, for this new little chick of our own. Everyone wanted to be a part of his room, and sent toys and clothes and wall hangings and music boxes. Letters and cards and flowers arrived daily. Jennifer wrote an amazing letter to her Godson, it arrived days after his arrival as promised, telling him how special he was and how special his parents were. She told him she herself was counting the days to meeting him, and couldn't wait to hold him at his baptism. This letter meant so much to me as in some special way it brought me peace. The three of us; Jennifer and I and this baby were in a circle together, and her letter let me keep that forever. I remember talking to her on the phone and she sounded tired, but I was so wrapped up in my baby, I only heard the joy in her voice. I discovered later that this was her intention; wanting to shelter me from any worry and leave me free to be in the baby world.

Jonathan's first few weeks were busy, but smooth, as he and I got used to each other, and we both got on the same crazy sleep pattern. I would sleep very little; too hyped with euphoria to want any down time. After feeding him at 3am, I remember sitting at the kitchen table, delighting in the bliss of quiet and no interruptions, as I sat and wrote. I wrote to family and friends; cards to thank them for sharing in our special time, and long letters to my sisters and friends at home in Ireland, to explain how I felt and how, 'my cup had indeed runneth over'. I remember my mother -in-law thought I was mad, she felt I should be grabbing the hours of sleep, but it brought me so much comfort to write the feelings down. I also at that time started a journal for Jonathan, and began to write in it for him, recording all the excitement his arrival had caused. This is something I would continue to do for the years to come; I recorded as we went. May rolled around and we had our first Mother's Day, it changed the whole day for me to have my own baby. I talked to my mother and my mother-in-law. I had sent a "Happy Mother's Day to My Godmother", card to Jennifer, enclosing more pictures, and when I talked to her that day, she told me it was on her table beside her. Everyone who came to see her was required to look at the pictures of her godson, and be full of admiration. I also got my first card from Jonathan and his Dad and we all three felt the love that day.

Chapter Thirty-Six

Only a week later, I had a call from Jennifer's dad, telling me she hadn't been doing so well. I don't remember taking it too seriously, and I prayed that she would get better. I told her dad I was thinking of both of them, and that I would call the next day. However, when I got off the phone, I called my husband, and said I had to go see her. I couldn't fly because I would need to bring a lot of stuff for the baby, and also, at that time, we didn't even have a credit card so our financial situation influenced the decision. I decided to go by train. It would take eight hours. I decided to surprise Jennifer, and all the way there, I saw her face when she would see the baby and hold him for the first time. I remember thinking of calling at the stop in DC, but decided to just go with the original plan. I was on a train with my six week old child; stressed with how to feed him, change his diaper and keep him content, and the phone was just too complicated. We continued on the journey and the baby slept. All I could think about was getting there.

My older brother met my train, and wanted to go to his house for us to rest first. I said, "No please, let's just stop, even briefly, and once I see them, we can go to your house". He brought me to 91, and I saw the police cars with the lights flashing and knew something was up. Jennifer's Dad saw me arrive, and when I got out of the car holding my baby, he had walked toward me with Jennifer's aunt, and then they were on either side of me. He told me Jennifer had passed away, just a short while ago. I remember feeling shock and disbelief. I would hold myself together, because this was her father standing in front of me. I knew, more than anyone else, the special love, bond, charm these two had for each other. Jesus Christ, I remember thinking, "what kind of sick joke is this. She never got to see my baby, hang on! She is the Godmother....oh God! Jennifer, I let you down; not here in time, didn't even tell you I was coming". I felt so stupid.

The only comfort that I had, as time went by, was in knowing for sure, in my true heart, that Jennifer knew how much I loved her, and that she really wanted me to enjoy my own new arrival. I stood at the top of the Auditorium a few days later, as we all gathered to say our goodbye's, and paid tribute to her in the only way that I knew. With my words, and my voice, and I felt that I was echoing her words and her voice. I reminded everyone of the kid who got excited about it all, the kid who was a friend, the kid who adored her father and couldn't wait to call him and tell him all her news, the kid who had been in my life and who I would miss.

I left my baby with my sister and drove over on my last morning, before returning to Virginia, and cooked an Irish breakfast for Jennifer's Dad. We both sat and chatted, and the very fact of sitting at that table brought me comfort. We would miss Jennifer greatly. Her Dad assured me that he would step up and be a Godparent in Jonathan's life. I smiled, thinking Jennifer would like that. There was nothing to say, except reassure each other that we would stay in touch, and we have.

Chapter Thirty-Seven

I returned home to the comfort of my small family; the three of us cocooned each other, and life went on. In a couple of weeks, Memorial weekend of 1995, family and friends gathered again, for Jonathan's Baptism. I remember going to the church to set it up, and being shocked at how hard I had to push to get the priest to understand how this was something we all wanted to be a part of. He was fascinated by my assuming that all baptisms were like this. He seemed surprised at my wanting to personalize the readings and the prayers of the faithful. This was my first time to realize how much my faith and values were based on the Irish experience, and that it could be different. I guess I had taken for granted that openness and involvement; the faith heritage from my father, it was what I grew up with. After discussion and some persuasive talking on my part, it was agreed that it could be worked out. We had a beautiful ceremony, reminiscent of home, no surprise!

The only missing piece was Jennifer; I thought of her all through the day, and found comfort in knowing that she would have loved the whole event. My brother Fintan was there as Godfather, and my older sister was Godmother. We sang hymns and said prayers, and this child was so loved and so welcomed that I felt truly blessed. My husband's family all came and it was wonderful again to all be together. My sister and her family travelled from up north and this especially surprised us, as her own new baby girl was only a few weeks old. We partied afterwards at home, and took enough pictures to mark the event forever and keep the memories safe.

While I had been away earlier in the month, my husband had started researching the process of buying a house. He couldn't wait to share it all, and let me know that it was actually possible. I thought he was crazy. I didn't want any more change; I just wanted my simple days back, and to be with my baby. He left it alone for about a month, but on drives out together, on the weekend, we would accidently/ on purpose drive in front of a property with a, 'For Sale', sign. I slowly opened up to the idea and we went through the process of looking seriously, and we very quickly found a house where we could both see us living. It was small, only 1200sq feet, but it had a deck at the back and a beautiful green sloping lawn also, that ran back to meet the numerous trees that were like woods at the edge. It was on a quiet street, a few minute's drive from my husband's work, and a very convenient location. We packed up and boxed and crated all our belongings and moved in on a very wet August night, with the help of friends who resorted to black garbage bags to keep the rain off!

We settled in very quickly, and this house will always be a reminder for me of Jonathan's first steps and his first words, and lots of other firsts that we all watch for with our children. Our days were peaceful and fun. He and I would walk around the yard, and find slugs and bugs and butterflies. He would follow behind his dad, pushing his own pint sized mower, to cut the grass. We took trips to the library, and came home, sat side by side, and we discovered and uncovered the mysteries within the covers. He loved Little Bear and singing, and I would find myself looking at him, and marveling at the luxury of all of this time, just us. He would stand on a chair beside me in the kitchen and arrange the apples in a pie dish; he had his own mini mixer and his own mini pans. I would tell him of my mother and grandmother, and our baking sessions when I was growing up, and he would listen in awe of a story that he doesn't yet know will lead to him.

Life went on around us, and he and I joined in or not, depending on our plans for the day. My husband continued happy and satisfied with his job, his reputation was growing and also the workplace's appreciation of him. I too, at this point, remember being more appreciative, especially of being a stay at home Mom and it seemed we had both found our niche. It was a wonderful experience; to be so happy living such a simple life and for all three of us to feel so content.

Chapter Thirty-Eight

Two events marked 1996, the first being a visit from my parents. They came to the States from Ireland, and visited each of us in our newfound homes. They arrived thrilled and excited to see Jonathan, and left me with memories to treasure. My memory holds pictures of Jonathan walking side by side with my father, as they set off together to explore the neighborhood. It was fun to see my young son pointing everything out to his grandad and giving a running commentary as they went along. It was a joy to see my mother and my child reading, and talking about the words and sharing with each other what they saw in the pictures. It was a great visit, and I saw them seeing me with my husband and child, and I was happy. My mother and I sat on the deck, out back, and shared in the simple life and how little it really takes to make a person happy. I saw acceptance and gladness in them, and I myself was happy to show off my independence through this new family I had created. They saw my husband as he truly was, and knew that we were meant to be together, but also, good for each other.

In the year and a half since Jennifer's death, I remained in close contact with her Dad. We continued to keep her in each other's lives and memories by talking about her with each other. We remembered, as we always would, her birthday and the day before her birthday; all the days that brought her closer. In the summer of '96, I remember a call from him, and feeling afterwards that he had something to say, but didn't get to it. I knew he would come back to it. A few days later he called again, and slowly told me that he was seeing someone, and that they had decided to get married. I was ecstatic and told him so, and also how thrilled Jennifer would be, reminding him of her mantra, "Get a life, Dad!" A few minutes after my chat with him, the phone rang again and it was his future wife; we had a lovely chat, it was so kind of her to include me and to want to share their plans. Of course I called him back, and we were a mutual admiration society reaching across the States. They got married in September and it is my regret to not have been there. Our own lives, at that time, were so self-contained; a trip four hundred miles north, with my small son, was too much. I can only know that they knew we were with them in spirit and offering one hundred percent support. They came together to see us that fall, and it was bitter sweet, but my overall feeling was one of gratitude to see Jennifer's dad have the chance to hold hands with someone again, and be so happy.

In 1998, Jonathan was three, and we had enrolled him in various activities, to give him the chance to be around other children. I had had another miscarriage the previous year and we knew that he was destined to be an 'only'. My own circle of people expanded, and naturally included other mothers with children, the same age as mine. We gathered for play dates and 'Mommy and Me' events. We went to music classes, and afterwards danced afternoons away together with the volume turned up. He moved on to preschool and a little more structure and he thrived. We began to see that with new interests and activities we were running out of space. He needed a playroom, and so did his mother! To be able to be less restricted; to build and create and have friends over. It was getting a little old to be constantly moving something to make room for his next activity.

Chapter Thirty-Nine

We put our house on the market, and went looking. Again, Divine Providence came to our rescue, and we met a builder on our search, and he had a house for sale. We went to look at it and loved it. It would mean more space, a great yard, and the house was in a rural setting which really appealed to us. We explained our dilemma, with a house to sell first. He solved the problem, by buying our old house! And that's how our new home came to be.

Once again, we packed and boxed, and once again, I had my sister on hand to help. We moved most of it ourselves and I remember walking in with a lamp in one hand and a bag of toys in the other. The neighborhood was idyllic. We had a five mile stretch of road, leading out from town; chickens crossing and cows grazing in the fields. There were flowers and shrubs and lots of trees. It was country, it was home, and once again, I had echoes of my beloved places from Ireland.

We settled in, and life took on a new rhythm. Jonathan was busy and curious, and loved to be out and about. I remember going for walks with him down a nearby road; with him riding his tractor and totally in a world of his own.

He would talk and tell me everything he saw and I would find myself looking and wondering how I had missed seeing it myself. He had friends over and they rode their tricycles around; safe in a neighborhood so far from town, and the traffic. We sat and wrote letters to his uncles, aunts and grandparents; filling them in on his life and busy days, and getting them ready for when he would visit. I talked to him about everyone; keeping them a part of his life even though they were so far away. If we did something that reminded me of anyone at home, I shared it with him, wanting him to feel a part of my memories, and so a part of the people too.

That first Christmas, in our new house, we had all my family living in the States come and celebrate with us. It was a wonderful time of sharing, and catching up, and looking back and looking forward, and marveling at where we were. As usual, traditions from home were central to the celebration and we continued to blend the old and the new.

We attended Mass together, and thought of everyone at home doing the same thing. I felt teary eyed listening to Christmas carols that transported me to the Cathedral of my childhood. We observed all of our holiday traditions, and I remembered my Grandmother especially, and felt nostalgic in my memories of the farm. Everyone was busy searching for what they needed, and it was a treat to be together and just be; being comforted by each others' presence. We told ourselves that we had created a fairly good reproduction of the holiday season of our childhood, and we all returned to our regular lives with the reassurance that it was possible and we could do it again for many years in the future.

Chapter Forty

Around this time, I started to think about going home. Back to Ireland! It was 1999, and so twelve years had passed. It had crossed my mind, obviously, over the years, but never in any serious way. We were so involved and busy getting on with setting up our own lives, that to interrupt it wouldn't have worked. So, I was a little surprised to have such strong feelings about a trip, and started to talk about it, more and more. Finally, I put the words together one night and said to my husband, "I think I want to go home", and his response was, "I know". So, Aer Lingus got a call, and suddenly it was happening, Jonathan and myself were on our way with plans in place. I colluded with my older sister, Jonathan's God-Mother, and she agreed to keep it a surprise. I had no second thoughts and just wanted to pack the cases now! And so, when the time rolled around, we were so excited it was almost tangible.

I planned to drive to New Jersey, visit with Jennifer's dad and his new wife, leave my car with them, and they would take us to the airport. It worked beautifully. It turned out to be a perfect interim in time; to share the anticipation with the only people who could possibly understand. I remember walking toward the departure gate at the airport, and Jonathan turned in his stroller and shouted, "I love you" back at them, as they waved us off. The flight went smoothly, and upon arrival, we delightfully listened to the pilot make the announcements. The welcome was a mix of Irish and English. I was overcome with nostalgia and also fright. It had been so long since I had been here I was feeling a little anxious! I reassured myself by looking at the evidence of my new life; my small son. Before long we heard the details for landing and the Irish weather forecast for that day; calm, showery, a little overcast and some sunshine. As I smiled at the predictability of the weather, I heard, "Failte/Welcome and enjoy your visit to Ireland". I remember looking at Jonathan as I continued to smile and thinking...... YES, only in Ireland and I am indeed home.

My sister was waiting when we got through customs and had picked up our luggage. What a reunion! We had remained good friends; she herself had been in the States for many years and had returned to Ireland in the past year. But it was different to be back here and we both knew it. We drove from the airport at Shannon, on through Tipperary, and Golden and Cashel, and then we were almost there. We looked out the window and inhaled the glory beyond. It was so strange to be back. At the same time so delicious. My emotions were all over the place, and I got my first inkling of that brewing confusion; am I Irish or American, or both?

My parents had built a one level house, located outside the town, and this would be my first time there. Perhaps this gave me a healthier perspective; they and their lives had moved on too. My sister had told them some American friends of hers were coming, so lunch was all set. The big surprise was that it was me and my son. It was memorable and tearful, and like an out of body experience. My father threw his arms about me and hugged me, as he said, "You're a right one, I never thought you'd come home again". And then he picked Jonathan up and they were both crying. I made my way to my mother, she was standing behind him, and we held each other; both thrilled to be there.

Lunch followed, and lots of conversation and catching up. Then we said Goodbye, as we were staying in my sister's house; an adorable country cottage that was straight out of a book! I knew that my mother, especially, was disappointed that we were not staying with them. I needed this space; to be able to hang on to the wife and mother in myself, and to keep the established healthy distance from the unpredictability they continued to represent. They understood that I wanted to be at my sister's house, and that many all night conversations would follow. I agreed to come and stay a night, so my mother could spoil her grandson, with a special dinner and breakfast too.

Arriving at my sister's we collapsed in exhaustion. A cup of tea revived us and hours of conversation followed. Jonathan has, meanwhile, explored her country house and the horses in the field behind it. I am so filled with the joy of being here that I could burst. I want to see so many people, and show off my little Yank! That night we sleep so well, and wake up the next morning with lots of requests for our time. I drive out the driveway and have driven a few miles on the wrong side of the road! People are waving at me, and I think they are just being friendly. I have to rein myself in and slow down. Everything is calling me, from the scenery to the people out walking, to the food I know is being put on the table.

Lunch with my parents, and afterwards I stand at the kitchen window and my mother and I watch, as my father and my child walk hand in hand around their yard. She thanks me for coming home, and she still can't believe I am here. We settle on an evening to stay at the house, and then I am eager to go see everyone else. I go into town to see the rest of my family. My younger sister, having returned from the States, has purchased our old home, and she and her builder husband have done an amazing transformation. She has her own business now; a deli/bakery and it all looks shining, new, and the perfect place to display her delicious baked goods. We enjoy more tea and home goodies, and chat, and as will be the case with all my visits, I feel the sadness of such a short time here. I fill every minute though, and remind myself that I can return again, any time.

We spend a day in Cork, with another sister, and Jonathan splashes his way around Blarney Castle in his rubber Wellington boots and looks so at home it brings tears to my eyes. Everywhere we go, there is a great welcome, and I want to box it up and bring it back to the States with me. One day we go with my mother to visit her sister, and more tea and chat and trips down memory lane follow. I drive around the countryside, in awe and seeing it under the influence of my twelve years in America. I ask, "Which am I, Irish or American?" This question arises many times, silly really, but a little confusing to feel this way here, and know and love my life at home in the States too. We visit the convent, where I went to school, and they see my child and tease me about the American accent, mine! It's a wonderful feeling of connecting though, and I will always remember one of my nun friends asking about Jonathan, "and does he know how to bless himself". I remember laughing so hard at this; it was so Irish and so funny. I wanted to say to her, "because I left and went to another country, I didn't leave my faith and my central core self and get lost in the mix". My child would always feel a connection to God, and develop his own faith, having seen and been around mine.

We drove to my grandparent's farm, and I had my moments of being still and remembering. Back in the actual place is a little different to talking about it. You almost see the people, and it's fascinating to see a wall or a gate, still in the same place. I also went by the cemetery, as I drove toward Cashel, and took pictures of the headstones to take back to the States. I remembered the days that the burials took place, and again it was a surreal experience. To see my own mother mourn her parents, and try and get a grip on the sadness. It only reminded me that we share more than we know, or want to think about, and that the cycle of life is indeed self renewing; as ultimately we all go through the same loss.

We spent a day at the beach, two of my sisters came with us and it was great to remind each other where the old haunts were, and which still existed. We walked by the cliff and saw the rock pools in the distance, and the flag flying red to deter swimming. Jonathan roamed the beach and stuffed his pockets with sea-shells; he would pack them safely in his suitcase and bring them to put in the garden at home. We stopped at the bakery and ate chocolate éclairs and cream doughnuts, straight out of the box. This was a tradition that Jonathan loved sharing. We let ourselves be wrapped in the well being that the place inspired in us, and we drove home with a sense of renewed understanding, of why every last one of us loves the ocean. I would always try and include a trip here on future trips home; it was such a central place for my young life and I will always feel that because of that experience so many years ago, with my father, that the place has kept some little piece of myself to return to. I visited with my old school friend and we marveled at the time that had passed. We went out to dinner, while Jonathan spent some time shopping with his beloved Godmother, and she and I remembered our school days at UCT, and talked about our lives now. I share the details of life in the States and she comments on how happy I am, just talking about it. To mark my first trip home, she gave me a beautiful porcelain doll, with a mad head of red Irish curls. It has pride of place in my home, and over the years she has gotten some more to keep her company.

Our night to stay at my parents arrived, and we sat at the table with them and enjoyed a meal, that Jonathan would always talk about as a reference point for Irish food. He had his first taste of Irish ice-cream, and my mother's apple pie, and he delayed going to sleep as his cousins had arrived with my sisters. It was fun to put Jonathan to bed later and see that my mother had put a hot water bottle in for him and a teddy bear by his pillow. My Mother! My Child! Three generations under the same roof; it made me realize the blessing it was for me to witness this, and it was also a reminder of all the little things she did for us as children.

We both slept well, and the following morning we had our one and only traditional Irish breakfast. My mother had even made fresh brown bread, it reminded me of the farm, and again, my mother and her mother come together in the same memory. After breakfast, Grandad took Jonathan with him to the car wash, and my mother and I had a chance to talk. It was enough, and she and I both knew this was the start of a new way. I was fully in my new life now and we would all be able to move on. I felt a new appreciation for my mother; I guess at this stage I saw how difficult it would

have been for her, with so many children, from my own
vantage point of only one.

Our last day arrived, and we kissed and hugged goodbye,
and with tears in my eyes I turned the car towards the road.
The return trip was so completely different; as I got on the
plane, I could only think about landing and sharing, and then
going to Virginia for the reunion with my beloved husband.

Jennifer's dad met us at the airport, and we drove to
their house where we would stay over and drive to Virginia
the next day. I can still remember talking nonstop. I had so
much to say and so much to share. I am sure it must have
been at times entertaining to hear me talk so fast, echoing
what I had heard and seen and felt, over the last ten days.
We spent a lovely evening and then collapsed into blissful
exhausted sleep. The next morning we hit the road early,
we were anxious to be back in our own house. I remember
thinking that it had been good to have the chance to unload
so much of my Irish overload in New Jersey; otherwise I
might have completely overwhelmed my husband.

Chapter **Forty-One**

It was so good to arrive back in Virginia. We arrived at the house and straightaway noticed a major change; my husband had done some fabulous landscaping while we were away. Later, he explained it by saying that he wanted to surprise us, but also he needed to keep himself busy. He found it lonely while we were gone, and had missed both of us. Jonathan was almost as bad as me, and talked his Dad's ear off; filling him in on everything and everyone he had seen, and about the dinner Nana had cooked, and the delicious Irish ice-cream. For me, I had to go through a period of adjustment, to get back into life here. Not within my own small family, but certainly with everything and everyone else. I remember feeling resentful that nobody could possibly understand, how there was a certain 'giving up' of something, to continue to live here. I found this fascinating. I didn't actually verbalize it, I just thought it, and I thought it was an interesting way to perceive the whole situation. Years earlier, I had wanted to leave Ireland, and in fact couldn't wait to leave. Now, here I was, faced with the dilemma that I wanted some of what I had given up back. Oh, what fickle minds we have! I slowly allowed myself to reacquaint with all that I loved here, and promised myself that future trips would be planned, and I reassured myself that this feeling would pass.

The time passed, and my main way of telling that we were moving forward was by the changes in my child, as he got older. In March 2000, he turned five, and we, as his parents, had to come to terms with the fact that he was almost ready to start full time school. It was a scary time for me, and I realized that quite a few of my fears were based on wanting to give him a similar educational experience to the one that I had had myself, and wondering where I could find it. I let myself off the hook for a few months, and Jonathan and I resumed our life of days filled with music and walks, and stories and explanations. The day of registration arrived, in May of that year, and I chose a newly built school as my first place to explore. It was a public school and not too big. All three of us went for a second visit, we enjoyed our conversation with the principal, and Jonathan was especially excited to be doing Art and Computer. He would start the following September. He was ready, we just had to hurry up and catch up to him. It was hard, hard to see him go, because there are so many threats out there, and I wanted to keep my baby safe. I finally realized that, being an only child, the social aspects alone would be really great for him. My husband and I both knew we were doing the right thing, and on the first day of school, led him by the hand to meet his new teacher.

From that first day there, he was happy; he loved his teacher and found his first best friend. He was proud that he could already read, and loved all his new subjects. He loved his packed lunch and for the first while at least, homework was a novelty. It was good for me too; not every thought was focused on this child, and I had time to pursue my own interests. I started writing for the local paper, pieces about the value of family life and the basic ideals that we all, deep down, share, no matter your country of origin. I enjoyed it enormously, and I also used my extra free time to catch up with friends, without all of our kids. I indulged my love of books; at the library, at the bookstore, at the book exchange.

The holiday season was fast approaching, and we were looking forward to it, with lots of family visits planned. For Halloween, I remember Jonathan dressed up as a cowboy, his paternal Grandma from up north came to visit, and she went out with him, trick or treating. She got such a kick out of it; the Armenian in her experiencing this as a whole different custom. My husband's brother, closest in age to him, was now married and had a daughter, and they came for Thanksgiving. It was a fun Irish/Armenian/American gathering, and we ate all the traditional foods of the holiday. It was nice for Jonathan to see his baby cousin, and to see his aunt and uncle be amazed at all his new knowledge, now that he was in school.

Christmas tended to be my family time; we all wanted home and I was a sure bet by now for providing it. We had my sister and her son, who was only two years older than Jonathan, and they were great pals. Another sister and brother came from out of State, and we all snuggled in against the cold, and were warm just to be together. My husband loved all this entertaining, and looked forward to coming home to a big family dinner. We did the traditional holiday with Mass, and as always, this was followed by the cutting of the Christmas cake. Then when the kids were asleep, we got to work doing Santa. We filled stockings for everyone, kids and adults. If I didn't have a stocking on

Christmas morning, it was not Christmas morning. It's the memory of home, and all of us being excited that I want to remember and recreate. We arranged all the toys for the kids, assembled what needed it, and then had the inevitable cup of tea to round off the day. On Christmas day, there was the gathering around the table for Irish breakfast. I would have spent months beforehand, scouring the import stores for bacon and sausage, and whatever goodies they had. I would ask someone from home to ship what we couldn't find, if I felt we had to have it!

We all enjoyed this and inevitably, we would wonder what they were doing at home and this would lead to a phone call, and we might catch five or six of our siblings at my parents' house. After gifts, and being surprised by all Santa's bounty, we would settle in to play board games, while our dinner cooked. Again, an established tradition from my Grandmother's Christmas, when my Uncle Thomas would beat us at draughts. This was all simple entertainment and we loved every second of it. My husband would bring out the rummy and a couple of rounds of that would follow.

Dinner would be ready, and the smells alone were transporters and it was hard to remember whose kitchen and what country we were in. Following dessert of plum pudding and trifle, we would all be ready for a walk. The kids on tractors and bicycles and off we went to walk it off and talk and wander, and just be happy. Later, I would take a quiet time to read all my Christmas cards and letters; that has become a tradition for me since moving here. I love to hear from all my friends and family, and extended family, and I store them all as they arrive in the mail, to be opened at this special time, just for myself. There are always surprises within the letters, and reading them connects me back to

Ireland, in a way that nothing else can. I have always loved letters more than phone calls, because they can be re read.

The games continue into the early hours, and the Irish chocolates and other goodies from home round off the day, and before we know it, it's tomorrow and we have to collapse into bed; fully sated by a perfect day of what's ours and what went before us.

Chapter Forty-Two

The New Year, 2001, was quiet, it seemed like time had started to speed up and I remember thinking we are moving too fast. Jonathan continued to love school, and explore whatever came his way. That summer, we went to Ireland again, and I felt so much more sure of myself on this my second return. We visited Cork first, and my sister there brought us to Blarney again, and this time Jonathan kissed the Blarney stone; he officially had the gift of the gab. Like he needed any help! We went to Cobh and saw the Irish Heritage Museum; both of us fascinated at the stories of the Irish immigrants that had gone to the States before us. Here again, I felt the awareness of being Irish and American.

Another day, we spent time with my friend and her young son and it was such a novelty to be face to face, sitting at her kitchen table. It was a beautiful Irish spring day, and she and I chatted while our two sons played together, with cars and toys in the back garden. The last time we had spent time together our lives had been vastly different; full of the uncertainty of our life's path, but even then, we had been very conscious of the support we represented for each other. Now here we were, both happily married, each with a young son, and eager to chat about what the future held. I left her house feeling thankful for her friendship, and knowing that after my return to the States, we would continue to support each other.

We then travelled up to my parents' home and this time we stayed a few days. My mother joined us for day trips, back to the family farm and some nostalgia, and up to Clare to visit her sister. Going with her to visit this sister was something I had always done, and it had become an important part of the relationships I shared with her. They were only two years apart in age, and so alike in many ways, even though the lives they had chosen were vastly different. One had two children and one had twelve. It fascinated me though that these two women had grown up together, and that my beloved grandmother was mother to both of them. I loved going there; she always baked something delicious in anticipation of our arrival, and I loved to indulge. Even as I remember this, I am reminded that so many of my memories are based on food!   In Clare, on the way back toward Tipperary, we drove through Killaloe, and stopped to savor the rolling green hills that led to the lake, and walked around as if in a trance, amidst all this picturesque beauty.

We went, another day, to the beach, and both of my parents joined us, my father especially fascinated at how the memories appeared so clearly for me. "I can't believe you remember that", he kept saying, and I said, "I remember everything". Prophetic, indeed! It was a windy day, and we were nearly blown away as we walked the beach; I didn't care, it was part of the charm of the place. I was reminded of a day there, during one of our summer vacations, when all of us put on raincoats and rubber boots and chased each other down the beach. I guess it's as much a reminder of the uncertain Irish summer weather as it is of the different ways we enjoyed being there. Jonathan wanted to keep the tradition of the pastries so we stopped by the tea room for hot tea and scones, followed by our cream doughnuts. My baby wanted to bring a box home to his dad!

On the way home, we stopped, after passing through Cashel, and stood at the foot of the Rock as it was beginning to get dark, and the lights were awesome. There used to be a restaurant across the street, where my father would treat us to sausages and chips, returning home from late play on the farm. It was no longer there, so we continued on home, happy and replete with the magic that only a trip down memory lane can bring. I was more relaxed on this trip, more certain of myself and my own family; I had my son with me and my husband at home patiently awaiting our return, so the tourist in me felt free to enjoy the joys of the Emerald Isle!!

Chapter Forty-Three

We returned from Ireland, and I was busy getting Jonathan ready for the new school year. My husband was doing great; loving work and delighted with all the visits from his own family. While we had been in Ireland, his brother had come for a visit, so he wasn't so lonely. Jonathan went back to school after Labor Day, and little did we know what sorrow the nation would feel in just a few short days. The day of 9/11 will stay with all of us, and it is one of those days in history when everyone remembers where they were. I went to school and picked him up early, and we returned home and called friends and family; feeling the need to connect and be comforted. The next night, going to bed, Jonathan told me he didn't like his school anymore, as there was no God. I was shocked and wondered where he got the idea. I said, of course God is there. He mentioned asking the teacher to pray for the people that died, and she had said she couldn't. He thought she meant God wouldn't hear, because he wasn't there.

The next day, I went in with him, and the two of us sat in the gymnasium and prayed together. I let him pick the place, inside or out, as God was in all of them, and when we were done, he happily went off to his class. The sorrow for all the people lost and their surviving relatives was so prevalent, and I think brought all of us to think not only of our own families, but of the transitory and unpredictable nature of life in general. I felt personally that I had a new appreciation for all the people in my life. I vowed to put people first and continue to make the effort to keep the relationships so special to me, both here and in Ireland, alive and well. I was also profoundly touched by the empathy of my six year old son, and his need for divine comfort in such an inhuman experience.

Chapter Forty-Four

In early 2002, after a holiday break spent talking and exploring options, my husband was almost ready to take the leap required to open his own store, and I was almost ready to support him. We decided to think seriously about this, and would use his Mondays off every week to explore the areas of town and maybe see what was available. During his time working at his old job he had met, and become friends with, an Armenian guy, named Richard, who would become a very good friend. We called on him to help us explore some ideas, and he helped us out by calling and letting us know if some property, that he knew was available, might be of interest to us. We also checked the newspapers, and went to auctions or estate sales that we thought might have items we could use. We stored it all in our garage and watched it pile up. We checked every available rental space in the town over a two week period. Most we could rule out immediately; no water, no gas link, or too many stairs.

My husband's vision was a luxurious, welcoming space for the showroom, with a larger space to house all the machinery and supplies for the workshop. We had no luck but we continued to look. He left his current job in early

March, and we had a goal of being open by May 1st. March came and went, and still no premises. I remember being at home, after dropping Jonathan to school, and my husband calling, very excited. He had found a property and needed my opinion, "I think this is it, please come and meet me, to look at it". I flew across town and met him there. It was a nice location, with trees and shrubs and lots of nice landscaping. The place for us to consider was on the 2nd floor, and when I went up to check it out, I knew he had found our starting place. There were other offices downstairs, but we had the 2nd floor to ourselves. We signed a lease the same day, and had four weeks to get it set up as a store. I remember a mad scramble to check with the county office re zoning regulations. We needed confirmation that it was approved for commercial use, and this was a legitimate query, as all the surrounding offices were just that; for dentists, attorneys and other non- retail businesses. We got the all clear. Yes! The zoning allowed for retail so we could go ahead.

It was the most insane time in my memory. We had no income coming in, bills were still arriving and it seemed like every day there was more going out as we purchased what we needed for the new space. We watched our money carefully and the savings got us through, but it was very scary as we lived through it. We used to reassure each other that it would all work out; we both realized that if we didn't give it a try we would always wonder. I remember the excitement of our 1st day, it was just myself and my husband and 1 other employee. My husband had trained her in his previous job, and they had worked together for seven years; she had left that business six months before him. We had stayed friends, and she was so excited at the idea of being with us in our new venture. We advertised in the local paper, and we sent out flyers in the mail. We knew my husband had lots of followers and supporters, but we needed them to know where to find him.

We got a lucky break one day, the local paper had come out, and someone was asking if anyone knew where x the jeweler went. And there were lots of replies and lots of free advertising for us, and before we knew it, we were up and running and the business went in leaps and bounds from there. It was a very exciting time. My husband designed and created unique pieces, and before long we had lots of showcases to display the new merchandise. They worked every day and only stopped to deal with a customer. The phone started to ring and we got busier and busier. My husband and I would go out on the weekend, and inevitably run into someone who was wondering where he was, and we gave them the new address and word of mouth spread it around.

My job was to keep track of the paper trail; check and pay bills, record the inventory and file taxes. I also loved to chat with customers and get to know them, as they waited for my husband to design for them. I did the bank deposits and the mailing and anything else that turned up. We loved working together. It was the perfect arrangement; I would leave early afternoon to pick Jonathan up from school, and take him home and deal with homework and all that. Our first Christmas was a lot of both fun and stress; we did enough business to know that this was viable. We were very excited to close the door on Christmas Eve, knowing that continuing with it in 2003 was now confirmed.

Our one year lease was up on May 1st 2003, and the owner, who had an office himself on the first floor, told us in February that the building was going on the market. We were floored, we had worked so hard to let everyone know where we were, it was a perfect out of the way location for us, and how could we start all over again? It was tough to know what to do. I remember sitting at dinner that night, and suddenly my husband said, "Why don't we buy it?" We spent 24 hours gathering up the financial information we would need for a mortgage, and got pre- approved the next day. We went to chat with the owner, we could tell he was surprised, but delighted, and we signed the deal the same day.

We couldn't believe it; we had all this extra space now, and could do whatever we liked with it. We knew we would not rent any of it out; we could use the space to its potential by knocking a couple of walls etc, and so the original dream would really come to life. We wouldn't close the deal and take possession until mid April, so there was little we could do, but there was a huge relief in knowing that we wouldn't have to look for a new location; our business had found a long term home.

Chapter Forty-Five

The year 2003, was memorable for a much sadder reason, and it was a sad event all my family wished could have been avoided. I was having a regular day, it was the middle of March, savoring the idea that our plans for the business were moving forward, and thinking of the possibilities ahead. My phone rang, just as I was thinking that I would have to leave soon to pick Jonathan up from school. I knew it was an Irish call, and I remember looking at the clock; it was 3 o' clock or 8pm Irish time, and I had about twenty minutes to chat. It was my older sister and I got ready for our usual chat. I was not prepared for the next words out of her mouth. "Fintan is dead". I remember feeling shocked, and saying, "What"? She said it again. I asked when and how, and stood holding the phone, mentally calculating even as we talked, how quickly I could get home. She told me he had died by suicide; he had hanged himself. All I could say was, "OK, thanks for calling me, and I will see you soon". I remember it was a Wednesday. After I hung up, I said, "Please God, take care of him".

I called my son's school and asked that he be ready to leave with whatever he would need, as we would be away for a month. I called my husband and he immediately

163

knew something was wrong, and when I told him he was as shocked and devastated as I was. My next memory is a call to Aer Lingus, and I booked from JFK on the Friday. I cursed living in Virginia; we were so far away from a major airport. I couldn't get a connecting flight that wouldn't include hours hanging around the airport in NY, so my husband said he would drive us up. That night and the next day are a blur, as I talked to all the family here, and in Ireland, and none of us could think of anything, except getting home, and being together. We were all in shock, and trying to keep the sorrow at bay, until we made it out of here.

I couldn't sleep, and packed suitcases and sorted the business and the house mail etc, and on Friday morning at 5.30am, I knew, without a doubt, that I wouldn't be able to handle this by myself. I dialed the # for my Dr. in Dublin. I had talked to him the previous night, and he had shared my sense of loss with empathy and understanding, and offered support as I got ready to be in Ireland. I remember asking him, in the early hours of that morning, to give me a quote or something that I could focus on, to help me get through this. He asked if I could call back, I said "no, as we are leaving now for an eight hour trip to New York". After that, we had the flight to Ireland. He quoted a prayer to me over the phone and it brought me comfort. I thanked him and said I would call when I got into the same time zone. We drove that day, all day, heading to JFK, my husband driving. I kept repeating the prayer that I had written on an index card to keep close, it kept me focused, and able to take the steps that would bring me closer to home.

We said goodbye to my beloved, and I so appreciated that he had driven us, but at the same time, felt bad that he had to do the return journey alone. I arrived in Shannon and my sister was there. I walked in shock, felt shock, and thought that we will never be the same again. We got to my parents' house, and it was full of people; relatives and friends. We all hugged and I left shortly afterwards to go see my brother and say Goodbye. Jonathan and I stood by the coffin, looking at him all dressed up, and thought Jesus! What the hell is this? I could find understanding, but it was so hard to know and face the fact that I would never see him again. I wonder if he had thought it through, that he was leaving the other eleven of his siblings behind, or was he so far removed, that it wasn't a thought he could have. Jonathan put a drawing in, and I put a note telling him how much I loved him, and how sorry I was that he was gone and that I would miss him every day, for the rest of my life.

That night, we all stood in line, as people passed through to pay respects and offer condolences. I saw faces I knew; friends of all of us and each of us and it went on from 6pm until close to midnight. Then the coffin was closed, and my brother was carried out, and we would follow the procession to the church. As we drove through the town there were police officers on every corner and at every intersection; saluting and offering support. We got to the church, and another crowd spilled out and onto the street. We all followed each other and took our places at the front. The altar was packed with priests from all over the diocese, and priests who had served in the parish when we were growing up. I found this particularly touching, as they had all been transferred out to different parishes, and here they were, back to offer support. I remember a prayer, and more people coming in and up to us.

Then it was time to leave, and go home and try and sleep.

I stayed at my parents' house; I needed to stay close to my mother especially, and try and be there to offer her comfort. It was hard and we sat at the table and she shook her head and told me all that had happened, and asked what could she have done differently to help him? I couldn't even begin to go there. I was too much in grief myself and unable to do anything, except let her talk. My father was the same; completely baffled.

The next morning, we gathered at the church for the funeral Mass. My brothers had spent the previous night choosing prayers and songs, and putting together a booklet that was a tribute to who my brother had been. All eleven of his siblings would have a part in the goodbye and we would each share in the service. The church was packed, inside and out, and again there were a great number of priests. The Bishop was in attendance, out of respect for my father's position and involvement in the church. It was emotional as we all took part in this last step, and we paid tribute to our brother who had suffered through his life, and whom we all valued and would miss. We all got comfort from the friends that showed up for all of us.

When the Mass ended, we made our way to the cemetery, my father and my child holding hands as they followed the coffin, and there was a respectful stop outside the original family home. I thought my heart would break, as we all did, and we continued on, and parked the cars and followed my brother to his final resting place. I spoke the final words at the gravesite, as we all stood side by side, feeling a profound sadness and knowing we were all changed forever..........................

"All twelve of us are our own people, but the links that hold us together are strong. Each of us knows we can count on the others, and Fintan knew this too. All of us shared Fintan's pain and his joy; we all have our moments to remember. The one very obvious gift that we share, apart from the gift of each other, is the gift of faith, a strong faith that serves us well. Fintan's faith was simple and personal, not freely shared. The Catholic faith has rituals that offer comfort at a time like this and all of us, as we sat last night with him, and greeted so many people, felt the love and the sorrow of loss, enfold us. Fintan will always be with us, as we will always be with him. His legacy is tolerance, how much simpler and happier all our lives would be if we could take this legacy and make it our own."

In memoriam: Fintan Damian Cummins, RIP March 19th 2003 age: 31 years

After the funeral service, I declined to join the usual gathering at the local Hotel, as was the tradition. I had told my parents, earlier that morning at the house, that I meant no disrespect, but that I would rather leave after the cemetery, and that I would see them later that night. I went with a friend and Jonathan, to another town, where we had lunch and talked. I couldn't quite get over the surreal sense of it all. So much had happened in such a short time. I had left the States on Friday am, and here it was only Sunday.

The next day, I went with my mother, to my brother's house where he lived alone. It was about ten minutes drive from my parents' house, but very isolated, and couldn't be seen from the road. We walked in, and saw the spiral staircase where he had died, and my mother just shook her head. All his stuff was meticulously tidy, and I remember noticing that his dress wear was in dry cleaner bags, and all his shoes were polished and in shoe bags. I looked through his books and his music, just to remember my sense of him, and then I left. I did not go back there again; I couldn't, and if my mother had been in search of answers, I doubt she found them.

Two days after the funeral, we got a call from the Hospital where my brother had been seeing a Psychiatrist, and they had considered the family request for an interview, and would see members of the family who wished to come, the next day. I called my own Dr. in Dublin, and we talked about the service, and how hard it was to feel and be around so much sadness. He again reminded me of his being available and told me to call him after the meeting, but to be prepared, it could be pretty rough. I got off the phone giving Divine thanks; I could get a respite and perspective just by calling his number.

Four of us went with my father the next day, and two doctors were already seated when we got there. They seemed defensive to me at the time, and it was only later it occurred to me that they felt protective of my brother, and were happy at the chance to defend him, or at least state his case. One of them opened a file and stated factually, "Fintan spoke of abuse by his father and how he felt his mother could do nothing to defend him". I started to cry and heard my father ask, "Abuse? Define abuse". I said to him, "this isn't about you, this is an effort to understand Fintan; this is about Fintan". He didn't hear me, and continued in the mode of asking, "is there anything in there that talks of all the holidays, and all the clothes, and all the schooling and books and a lovely house, is there none of that". All the rest of us could do was cry and feel helpless, as the doctor explained the medical terms for my brother's depression, and what she felt was the root cause. I couldn't stay, and got in my car and drove to a priest friend's house, about forty miles away, and cried for the rest of the night. He could do nothing but sit there and listen, as I talked my way through the pain. He told me that my brother had obviously reached a point where nothing could have helped him, and the impulse had won out. All we could try and do was remember our good times, and try and find some way of honoring him, by living. This helped me and I could at least go back to my family the next day, and not feel so consumed by it all.

My child was safely with his Godmother, and when I had called her, she said that she was ok, and that Jonathan would be fine with her, until the next day. It was the next day, that she and I and Jonathan, decided to take a few days, away from the crowds still arriving to pay their respects; and we headed north and west toward Achill Island. I remembered being there years ago, but had forgotten that the landscape was so barren and wild. As we drove toward Castlebar, we got a preview of what was ahead.

We passed the open fields on either side, with the sheep wandering, right into the road. We slowed down automatically, sensing a different pace. Houses scattered here and there, all well away from the road. I couldn't help but wonder what it would be like in winter, with the waves from the Atlantic crashing onto the beaches, and the rocks, and the spray, and the mist, being carried up onto the roads. I could feel the wind and the cold, just thinking about it. There wasn't a shop for miles; this was indeed beautiful, and natural and raw, but it took a certain type to survive it, maybe they were born to it and knew nothing else. We crossed the bridge from the mainland over to Achill and slowed down even more. The tide was out, and the beach lay open in front of us like a giant table. It was misting rain, and the sun was trying hard, and we saw a rainbow, and resisted the call of the ocean drive and found our hotel instead. I can still see Jonathan, my eight year old American! Talking on the phone to his Dad back home, telling him he was looking out onto the front lawn of the Hotel, and that he could see sheep grazing, "right here in front of me dad". He loved it, and within minutes had his Wellington boots on, and had crossed the empty road to splash in the puddles and pools left by the receding tide. We enjoyed dinner at the hotel that night with a fire lighting and traditional music in the background. My sister and I, quiet, as we allowed the peaceful, barren and desolate place to bring us comfort. We slept to the quiet and the ocean, and woke up the next morning, ready to explore.

We found the local shop with the standard Island sign of, 'Gaeilge agus Failte'; Irish spoken and welcome, and went in happily to stock up for a picnic lunch. We got sausage rolls and bacon wraps and plastic cups of tea, and headed off, as directed, to the Stone village. We stepped back in time, as we saw these stone huts inhabited, with openings for a window and a door, and a space dug up behind for a kitchen garden. We wandered along, going nowhere, and nowhere to go; just a vista of nature everywhere we looked. We surveyed the hills and the ocean, and the green grass stretching as far as we could see, with little dots in the distance to mark the cottages of the locals. We sat in the grass and ate lunch, and took pictures of each other, and the contentment of being so far from the sorrow that continued back home slowly enfolded us. We savored the silence, knowing no need to talk, and remembered and were, just for us.

We drove along the coast, in awe of the perfection of the tiny beaches and coves created by nature, and left untouched by man. It was the most perfect place to be, simple and filling, complex and empty. After our few days there we were ready to leave, with a promise to each other and to the Island; we would be back. All three of us felt like we had been to another world, but we knew it was time to return to the one we had come from.

I stayed for another two weeks, during which time we went to a beach house in Kerry, and invited my parents to join us. I arranged this break because I thought we could all do with a change of scene, and still have the familiarity of the summer vacation spot, and the comfort of the sea. I remember getting ready to go that morning, packing the car in the front driveway, when my father arrived out with a bag. I asked if it would not fit in his own car, and he told me that we would all go in my car. I mentioned that he might want to drive while he was there and that he wouldn't be covered for insurance in my rental. This is when he told me that when he had dropped my sister at Shannon airport, earlier that week, he had gone into Hertz and given them his driver's license and had himself added to my rental. I was floored. I thought Jesus! Does it ever change; this constant need for control, the bloody cheek of him. I didn't want to make a big deal out of it, and I certainly didn't want to upset my mother, so all I said was, "to heck with it, let's go." I remember stopping wherever I felt like it, and driving the whole way myself. I was so pissed off. Later that night, when I talked to other siblings, their reaction was all the same, "you're kidding!" When I thought about it, I really wasn't surprised as this was classic for him. I guess what made it so hard to take was the fact that here I was trying to help them cope, and get away for a break, and even in the midst of all that had been going on, he was able to think that far ahead re the car! It was a reality check for me, and reminded me to never forget that he had no boundaries, and whatever my feelings, he still felt ok with telling me what to do. To top it off, he knew what he had done was sneaky; why else would he have arranged it, and then waited until departure day, to say anything to me?

I remember it, like it was yesterday, and as a result of that incident, I always remind the car rental people when I pick up a car initially, that I am and will be the only driver! I am sure they think I'm nuts, but I feel the need to anticipate and protect myself again! At the beach, the place where we stayed was in the town where we had all stayed as children, it helped, and it didn't. My mother cried and told me she would never engage in prayer again; she had asked for her child to be alive and kept safe and it hadn't happened. Any words of comfort that I tried to offer felt empty, and all I could do was stay close to her and let her know she had support. My father asked "why" over and over, and I couldn't take it. I would have to shake my own head and leave the room. We got through the time; my sister came down and we talked for hours, remembering the good times and sharing our own memories of our brother. She and I walked the beach, our two children exploring the rocks and caves ahead of us, reminding us of the days when we were children ourselves. We returned home, and a few days later, I would leave and return to the States.

When we got home to Tipperary, it being Saturday, we thought about going to church with my mother, and I checked times in the churches around, as none of us wanted to go to the Cathedral. I found one in Holy Cross Abbey, and that's where we went. It is a beautiful chapel; reminiscent of the monastery it once was, and beautifully restored. We found seats, and Jonathan went off to light his candles, as was tradition, for whoever he was missing; like his dad in the U.S. and his friends from school and home. The Mass proceeded and we sat when it came time for the sermon. When I heard the word, "Suicide", I sat up and paid closer attention. The priest was pointing out to the congregation gathered, how we should understand and be clear, that the act of suicide is a way of turning one's face from God, and the Light, and a moving away from the faith. I thought I'd be sick, and took a peep over at my mother and saw that tears were flowing down her face. I was furious, and prayed that whatever else he had to say, he would hurry it up, and that the Mass could be over.

Only my respect for the sacrament stopped me from interrupting, and I waited until the Mass had ended and most of the congregation had left. I continued to wait with my mother, for the priest to come from the sacristy. He came out, and I called him aside and said how offensive I had found the sermon. He knew who I was, and also of the circumstances of my brother's recent death. He had the cheek to tell me that my reaction was an emotional one, based on the recent loss. I was floored, and told him that this actually was so not the case. Perhaps my reaction was more pronounced because of the experience, but that my faith; my Catholic faith, was based on a loving God, and that he, as a priest, was showing a human judgment, and allowing his personal prejudice to taint his sermon. I could see he was stumped, and so anxious to get away, but I couldn't help myself, I was so incensed; before he left I told him that he should be ashamed of himself, and that I was ashamed to have sat in a church, and listened to him.

I controlled my fury the whole way back to the house, and went away by myself to walk around outside, after we got there. I looked up the number for the Bishop and called his house. I explained who I was, and about the sermon I had just heard. I also told him that it was offensive and cruel, to speak in such a callous way, from the altar. Guess what his response was? Why are you calling me? What are you bothering me for? I prayed, Jesus Christ! Is this for real? I said to him, are you not the local head of the Church, don't you care that this was in one of your churches tonight? I asked what is the Catholic Church, and what does it stand for? Is it not by, for and of the people? I told him I was a Catholic, and asked if he felt any sense of responsibility to me, as one of the flock. What about basic human empathy, in light of the family's recent loss. He was not capable of offering any sort of response; he did not want to be informed of material being dished up as a sermon, material assumed to be reflective of Catholic doctrine, in one of his churches. I was so disgusted, the fact that he couldn't offer anything appalled me; I lost all respect for the man and the office he was supposedly in a position to uphold. He hung up on me. I couldn't believe such ignorance.

Well now, aren't we alive and well, and so very sure of our congregations and of ourselves! I was so pissed off I was capable of anything that night. It reminded me of why so many people move away from the established Church; such blatant disrespect from its leaders is hard to swallow. It was galling for me that someone in this capacity within the Catholic Church could imply that I did not even have the right to converse about an issue, or presume a right to be heard.

Meanwhile, my mother is in the living room, telling my father that she'll never go back there! We had a long discussion on the reality of faith being personal, and that one self righteous idiot shouldn't turn us all off. The joke was on us however, as a couple of years later, this same priest became the head honcho of a 3rd level Theology College, promoted by that same bishop. I prayed that that particular priest had seen the light, or that the students gave him a run for his money! This was 2003, and many in the Church had not yet acknowledged the reality; that the days of sheep following the shepherd in the Catholic Church, were numbered, if not over.

The crisis that the Church faces today in Ireland, indeed also in the United States, is a direct result of this keeping the dividing lines in place; the clergy and the power on one side, and the congregation on the other. Visiting churches over the years of my visits to Ireland, it is obvious that the trend of non attendance at regular Mass is growing. People become more vocal and less in awe, and feel more inclined to search within themselves for what they want in their spiritual and faith life, instead of blindly following the generations that went before them. Faith has become more personal and informed. I imagine that the uncovering of all the behind the scenes crimes that were committed, has seriously weakened the general public's view of who exactly should be revered and respected. There are priests that promote and encourage this change and see it as the development of a stronger faith and way of life, but they are on the sidelines, and until the current crop of archaic bishops and heads have moved on, or are moved out, the Church will not benefit from the new generation wishing to be a part of, and included in, their Church.

After all of this, and the reminder of the narrow views in existence and being allowed to be promoted, I felt ready to go. I was upset by all this nonsense, and saddened by my mother feeling that her Church had deserted her. Then there was the hope, as we all indeed continue to hope, that all this talk of tolerance and change might spur some conversations nearer to home, as in my father's house.

I felt eager to be gone in one way, but in the broader personal picture nothing was resolved, and we had all waited for my father to say something, anything, but he didn't. We waited some more, but it didn't come, and we had to be realistic and realize it never would. I remember thinking that I couldn't deal with it anymore and I wanted to go back to my own life. I felt the need to protect my own sanity and I was tired of it all. He honestly still believed that all he had done as a father should have been enough, and he did not have the capacity to see it in any other light. His inability to see beyond the role of provider was still central to who he was. We should just stop waiting for the awakening, and make our own lives better and enough. I returned home, and I will never forget the relief and joy at seeing my husband waiting as we came through the arrivals gate at the airport. It was good to be home.

Chapter Forty-Six

I remember wanting to get straight back into the rhythm of my life, I wanted the comfort of the familiar and the predictable. I was so glad that Jonathan was back in school and among friends his own age. He was in the process of preparing for his First Communion and thank God we had that to look forward to, and also to distract us. As I had come to expect, there was a minor glitch with the preparation, when I didn't attend the parents' class of the children receiving. This shocked me; my Church was aware of my reasons for being out of the country. The Church office called and said that if I didn't make up the classes, then my child wouldn't be getting his First Communion. I was so offended and didn't waste any time trying to explain.

I went to see the Pastor the next morning, and told him that as a parent choosing to have my child take part in the sacrament, a parent who had directed this child to where faith was a central part of who he would become, I found it offensive to be told to take a class to understand the purpose of the sacrament. Thankfully, he understood that faith and this sacrament was not about a class, either for me or my child, and more a way of life.

This is a stand I would continue to take throughout

177

my child's spiritual formation, having little or no patience with Church bureaucrats who wanted everyone to fit into their own idea of what something should be. Faith would continue to be very personal for me, and I would never feel the established Church as essential, possibly because of my abuse by the priest, and also because of my father's involvement in the Church when we were all growing up. Of course the incident of the sermon at Holy Cross Abbey, and my subsequent delightful conversation with the Bishop during my recent visit to Ireland, didn't help either. Hard to show respect to something that has shown itself in such an undeserving light.

I got back into work pretty quickly too as paperwork had piled up while I was away and there was plenty to do. We were busy making plans for the new store space, and all that took time and energy also. I was happy to have my husband and my son, but not a day passed when I didn't have the sad thoughts of my brother's death, and it was hard work to just keep going. I resumed my chats and phone calls with my Dr. in Dublin, and over the next few weeks I was able to work through my mixed up emotions and feelings of being so helpless. We planned a gathering of family and friends for the upcoming First Communion, and that would help. We would all get to be together again.

The First Communion was held mid May, and Jonathan looked so adorable in his suit, white shirt and red tie. It was held in the same church where he was baptized, and we all leaned out of our pews as he marched up the aisle. All my family here in the States attended and my sister, his Godmother, travelled from Ireland and was here for him also. Jennifer's dad and his wife completed the ensemble, and other friends would join us at the house later. We had a lovely evening afterwards, just talking and sharing, and enjoying the good food. My sisters and I had made all the usual traditional Irish food, and everyone appreciated and enjoyed the effort. We found comfort in each other, and in a way the event served as a reminder of the good we all had and would cherish. My eight year old entertained us with his witty comments as he opened his cards and gifts. We remembered who was missing and tried not to be too sad.

It took a few months, and a lot of hard work, to get the renovation job done at the store. My husband called on his fellow Armenian, his good friend Richard, and he came every day to help supervise the renovations and offer support. If we needed a wood floor guy, Richard knew one, and he was there that night! The same if we needed an electrician or a carpet layer. We kept the store running on the 2nd floor, and everyone who came in during this time was really excited to see the finished result. Many a night, I would be home with Jonathan, and they would call from the store and say they were staying all night; getting the floors in or the walls painted. This was a very exciting time; every day something new was going on, we found the perfect desk, the perfect lamp and the perfect oriental rugs for the floor. Gradually, the place took on the look we wanted and the final touches were all that were needed.

The workshop was also set up, with a separate polishing room. On this level we had a kitchen and a bathroom, and upstairs, more rooms, and a 2nd bathroom. It was decided that I would keep my office upstairs and we installed the desk and filing cabinets and the computers. I had a beautiful big window, looking out onto trees and flowers, and I knew it would be a very comfortable place to work. We had room now to set up extra storage, especially for the overflow of supplies that didn't need to be in the showroom, and we knew it was all exactly right. We were so thrilled when June 1st arrived and we moved into the new space, almost exactly one year after we had rented the upstairs and started the business.

We held a sort of Open House to celebrate, and friends and family and customers came from all over the country. We received beautiful floral bouquets and cards, and from Ireland, my parents had shipped a framed drawing of the Cathedral in my home town; to bring blessings from there to here. It meant so much to me that they thought to wish us well in our new business; it still hangs on the wall above the desk in my office. We were busy that day, chatting with all the people who showed up, everyone admiring the new showroom and how elegant and welcoming it was. We had our new staff with us; we were now a team of four, and it was a great day reflecting the smooth transition and the year to come.

Chapter Forty-Seven

Around this time, with the store comfortably set up and running smoothly, I had some time to devote to finding a new school for Jonathan. The incident of 9/11, and his upset because of not being able to pray, had stayed on my mind, and I knew we would move him to a Catholic/Christian school, as soon as finances allowed. So I set about looking at what was available, going to see schools and meeting with various people. There was a Catholic school but it was very big, with a student body of over seven hundred, and when I went there I didn't feel anything of the familiar about it. I wondered, at times, if I was searching in vain, but I persisted, and then one day, I found what I was looking for.

It was a Christian Academy, with students attending all the way from Kindergarten to 12th grade. I loved the campus; beautiful grounds, plenty of green space and lush green sports fields. The building itself was newly built and had all the modern educational technical stuff, as well as a well stocked library and science lab. I set up an appointment with the Principal, and went along to meet her. Jonathan came too, and when we got there, she said we could take a tour first. We strolled around all the classrooms as she explained their policies, and the school's mission statement. I remember hearing singing, and as we approached a music room she opened the door, and we could hear the choir singing the Gloria. It was so beautiful; I heard echoes of my own Ursuline Education, and I knew my search was over. Something about the whole experience that morning told me this was to be his new school. He would start in September, and sometime in the next month, could come and visit a class for a day, if he so wished. I was thrilled to have this dilemma sorted, because Jonathan would never worry again about being able to talk to God; at this school, prayer would be encouraged.

Now that the school situation was sorted, and the renovation and rearranging at the store was successfully completed, I could stand back and take some down time. I realized that I had been keeping so busy, not just because there was so much to do, but also because I needed the distraction. I still felt unsettled and very far from my family in Ireland. After a couple of weeks of not being able to shake the sadness, I knew that if at all possible, I needed to go back. So we talked about it, and agreed that about ten days in August would work, and it seemed like a miracle to me.

I booked the trip, and Jonathan and myself set off again, and once the plane landed I felt such relief to have been able to do this. We based ourselves in Youghal; a beach town we had never been to as a family. I chose it unconsciously as a place with no memories, but with the comfort of the sea. We had stopped briefly at my parents' house, and persuaded my mother to come with us. My father would join us in a few days; there was a novena or something going on in the Cathedral that he didn't want to miss. The three of us arrived and went straight to the beach and marveled at the tranquility. Youghal was beautiful; totally untouched and devoid of the commercialism of other seaside places. We spent the next couple of days just being together, my Mother enjoying cooking for us, and Jonathan using his influence with the menu and delighted with the undivided attention of his mother and her mother.

I walked, by myself, around the town and enjoyed the old stone buildings and the cobbled street, and was in awe that it remained as it had always been. I walked to the harbor and watched the boats come and go, some on serious missions and others just to view the splendor. I allowed myself to miss and mourn my brother, and in my head, I told him how we all missed him and wished from our hearts that we could have helped. It was a peaceful time, and over the next few days I began to feel better. There is truth in the belief that family members of a suicide, especially siblings, all wonder with guilt at their right to be still living. I had struggled myself since March and would continue to, but the comfort I found in Ireland helped me to recover. For my own peace of mind, I came to accept that, for whatever reasons, this is what was meant to be, and I vowed to find something constructive and tangible to honor his life ....and I did, and it helped me to move on, with a way to keep him with me.

Various members of the family joined us for a day or a night, and we allowed the fun of meals and board games, and walks and chats, and the beach, to heal us. Jonathan went off with my father on their own walks, and they enjoyed the company of each other. Having set the precedent on earlier visits, of the style of communication with which my son had been raised, I had put guidelines in place for my father, so I felt comfortable with him and my son being together. Also,

I knew I had a child, even at aged eight, with a strong sense of his right to be heard and an intolerance of angry or rude words around him. As a three year old, he had pulled my father up for the way he talked to my mother, and I remember thinking, "Good for you," and that set the standard.

They went to the local shop for the newspaper, and the church to light a candle, and I could see how good it was for both of them. My mother and I chatted, and she too was finding some peace; I can't imagine the pain of losing a child, and in her own situation it was compounded by her memories of helplessness and inability to do what she wanted in the earlier days for her child. As the end of the trip drew near we all felt ready to leave, and we spent our last night at my parents' house. My sisters came with us to the airport, and we all hugged, giving thanks for the time spent together and the fact that we all felt, at least, a little better. Another crossing of the Atlantic, and there stood my husband; ready yet again to welcome us home.

Chapter Forty-Eight

After buying the building where the store was located, we knew that the location was now fixed. The business would continue here and while we might continue to change it, with further renovations or whatever, we would stay at this location. We had a forty-five minute commute from our current house to the store, and the same to get home in the evening. With Jonathan's school also confirmed we would not be tied to a school district, and so we knew we wanted to move again. We took our time with this choice, weighing up the pros and cons for all the possible locations. We knew for sure that we wanted to be only ten minutes from the store and we also knew that as usual we needed lots of outdoor space, and we wanted more square footage. And so the search began.

I did most of the looking, as my husband was busy in his workshop and at the store, and it took time, but I finally found something I knew he should join me in checking out. At this time my older sister was visiting from Ireland, and she and I had great fun driving around looking and taking notes. She was with me when I found the house and she agreed that it had everything on the list, and that my husband should see it. We set the appointment for 8am the next morning; Jonathan could join us before school, and all three of us could chat together as we did the tour. Within five minutes, we knew that we would be moving and soon! That afternoon, we put an offer on the property and made the deal, agreeing to close in thirty days.

Another round of packing and sorting followed, and I prayed to God, "please let this be the last time". Every time we moved, the job got bigger, as we had accumulated more stuff with more rooms to fill. The day dawned bright and early, with the doorbell ringing at 7am; the movers ready to load up. I dropped Jonathan to school, and drove my fully packed car in front of the moving van, and off we went. It took all day, and then some! Our friend Richard was there to help, and as I was busy at the new house directing the guys where to put everything, he went and got Jonathan from school. That night, I stayed up until the early hours, putting everything in place and making it home. My last labor of love was to set up my home office, and I enjoyed filling up all my bookshelves with my books. My sister had come with her son and helped that afternoon also, and she had set up the kitchen. We had all had dinner together before she set off for home a little earlier. The next morning, I woke up and stopped off at Jonathan's room on my way down the stairs; his room was empty! I stood looking out the kitchen window and there he was, swinging on the swing set at 7am! Well now! We were indeed home.

At the end of 2004, my parents came for another visit to the States. They stayed with us for a week and we enjoyed showing them the new store and Jonathan's school. My father especially loved the beautiful woodwork and unique design of the showroom, he had never seen anything like it, and now that he was here in person had a better understanding of what our vision had been. My mother loved to try on all the jewels, and she loved that everything was so unusual and not something she had ever seen before. She loved my personal collection also, and would sit with me at home trying all my stuff on. At Jonathan's school, they couldn't believe all the available space and how Jonathan, at such a young age, was being exposed to so many different academic subjects.

Almost ten now, he was an avid reader, a hobby he and I continued to share. He loved series of books, always knowing when he finished reading the one in his hand, there was a sequel waiting. He went for long walks again with my father, this time with Sasha, our new addition to the family. She is our four legged Yorkshire-Terrier/Poodle, a very spoiled tiny ten pound dog. The main memory of that visit for me is when we got both, or either, of my parents to take a trip down their own memory lane, and share it with us. My father, especially, had a great memory, and recalled all the jobs he had as a young boy in his teens, anxious to help his mother in any way he could. He spoke about all the changes he had seen in the town where he grew up, and how all his family had learned at a young age to stay with something if it worked, and only if it didn't, that's when you changed. He remembered his time at school, where you got a wallop on the head if you didn't do your homework, or pulled by the ear, out of your chair, if you were talking. I can still see the expression on Jonathan's face; pure shock. The very idea!

My mother then talked about her piano teacher rapping her knuckles with a pencil, and how if you didn't have the ingredients for your home economics class in your bag, you would be sent off to get what you had forgotten; to walk home, five miles out into the country! We laughed at this, because it most surely has changed, the very idea of any of this wouldn't even be on my son's radar, and all this reminiscing gave me food for thought. It started the little nugget in my brain, of an understanding of the experiences that they both had before they even met, forget had a family of twelve children. And especially I started to think of the influences that had formed who they were.

My mother and I spent her last few days here Christmas shopping. They had never visited this late in the year before and this was a novelty for both of us. We found some great surprises for all the family at home and she was delighted with herself to be so organized. I also made my Christmas cake early so she and I would enjoy doing it together in my kitchen. I remember how surprised she was at how clear my memories were of her own mother, and then she nodded her head as if having remembered; and thus reached an understanding, "you always spent a lot of time there".

This visit helped to cement my established sense of separation; I was beginning to feel stronger in my own life and no longer saw myself as primarily connected to my parents and their life together. My husband and I felt a strong sense of our own family and this time with my parents we were especially conscious of them as visitors. Perhaps they sensed my autonomy and were influenced toward a changing relationship themselves. They returned to Ireland that year and families on both sides of the Atlantic were ready early for the holiday season, having gotten it off to a good start together.

The New Year, 2005, arrived and our main focus those early months was getting the new web site for the store launched. It was a lot of work, and we needed lots of technical expertise and support. It was an exciting time; my husband producing new pieces just for the site, and experimenting with his camera to get the pictures just right. Taking photos of jewelry is a whole different ball game; angles and color and light, all need to be exactly right. While he was busy with this, I was writing the introductions and informational pieces that would be on the home page. He was in his workshop, and I was in my office, and many times, in search of each other, we would meet on the stairs and take a moment to appreciate the fun of working together. We were so excited to be launching the web site. It would take the business into a new realm, we were not too interested in actually selling off the web, but we thought it a great way to let so many more people know of our existence. The day we were launched was memorable in that the phone lines were hopping; we got so many calls from friends and family, impressed with how unique it was. We felt all our hard work and patience had paid off. Since then, of course, we take it for granted, but the sense of having done it together, with such a reliance on each other's talents, has stayed with both of us.

Chapter Forty-Nine

In April of that year, we knew my father was having a check up, in hopes of resolving some health difficulties he had been experiencing. It wasn't until a call, late one night, at the end of the month, that we realized all was not well. He had been diagnosed with throat cancer, and would be exploring his options. Updates would follow. All of this was a shock to every one of us; he had never smoked, never drank and walked insane miles every week, so we always thought of him as being the picture of health. I could hear in her voice that my mother was in shock, and trying not to think beyond today. I felt so bad for her; they were coming up to their 50th wedding anniversary, and had always relied on each other. Everything they did, they did together. I figured it would be pointless to worry too much, until we knew what we were dealing with.

In May, he started to have serious and obvious symptoms, and at the next appointment at a Dublin hospital, they gave him his options. He opted to fight with everything they were willing to do for him, and so plans for a surgical procedure were set in motion. It was a major strain, to be hearing all this via phone calls, and it got to the point where I couldn't think about anything else, and I hated the idea of not being able to support my mother. So, I booked a flight home and we went in early July.

It was a little different arriving in Ireland, knowing that I was heading straight to a hospital in Cork, where he had been admitted. We were feeling sort of without a base too, because we hadn't figured out yet where to stay. Not being a hotel person, I opted for an apartment thirty miles away; half way between the family home town and the hospital. That way, if he was discharged, it was still an ok location. That trip, our luggage got lost! So myself and Jonathan were feeling very sorry for ourselves as we headed south that morning. Even under these stressful circumstances we both took the time to enjoy just being there. We admired the beautiful picture perfect scenes we passed; the cows grazing, the horses wandering and the landscape dotted with farmhouses and barns. We were distracted by the urgency of our mission, and would not fully appreciate where we were until we got to the hospital, where hopefully some reassurance awaited us. I was a little happier after I saw my father, as he looked the same; the only difference was that when he talked, he sounded hoarse. My mother was so delighted to have all of us around her, and it helped to keep her spirits up and feeling positive.

We sat and caught up in the café and restaurant beside the hospital, and tried not to be too open about our fears. We all talked about how weird it felt to be so upset about it, given that we all had such serious unresolved issues with him. I guess when push comes to shove, it's all put on the back burner, and the humanity and empathy that's central to being human comes to the fore. This being in the hospital lasted only a few days, and then he was discharged to return home, and wait to be given the date of his surgery, which would be done in Dublin.

I remember being on the outskirts of Cork, driving toward our rented apartment, when the cell phone rang. My father was being released, and I could drive both of my parents to their own home. There was a sense of celebration leaving the hospital behind, and we were all thrilled and feeling blessed to be returning to Tipperary. Jonathan and myself were so relieved, as now we could feel like we were really home; we were done with the hospital and could resume our enjoyment of the lush green landscape and the freedom to drive around and visit.

That night, my mother asked me if I would stay the next week at their house as she needed the company, and she felt it was not all going to be smooth sailing for him. She also felt that having Jonathan around would be a nice distraction for my father. So we went to the apartment and picked up our stuff, happy to see that the luggage had arrived from the airline. Driving back to my parents' house we were happy. It was weird really, but we both felt it was exactly where we should be. Seated at my mother's kitchen table that night, eating tea and toast, we all gave thanks just to be home and prayed, Please Lord, let us get through this.

The next morning, I had heard my father coughing and coughing, and it all sounded very distressed. When I opened the door of the bedroom, my mother was standing in the hall and tearfully told me she had called the doctor, and he was on the way. My father was bleeding from his throat and having difficulty swallowing, even water. She asked me to wait at the front door and let the doctor in.

The doctor calmed him down, gave him a shot and explained to my mother this was not a serious or troubling development; that we all needed to realize that these incidents would occur, while he waited for his surgery. He had left a prescription for painkillers, so I went into town to pick it up, and when I returned my father was asleep and my mother had her head in her hands at the kitchen table, giving her sorrow free rein. I put my arms around her and tried to comfort her and thanked God to be there. We were ok after a while. We both acknowledged that this was harder, given my father's healthy lifestyle, and our own perception of him as being invincible. She agreed and was comforted by the reminder that he would be taken care of, and that this waiting time would be the hardest.

We stayed there for the week, and I couldn't say who I saw or what I did, it was a time to just be, and I am forever grateful for having had the chance to be close to my mother at that time, and offer my support. Jonathan, I remember, offered light relief; he was out wandering in the field behind the house, and came in to tell my father he had checked out the property. He sounded so serious and adorable. He sat with my mother, showing her his books and reminding her that he was a great letter writer; so she wouldn't miss him too much after he left. She made pancakes for him and put stewed apples in them and he thinks of them every time I make pancakes at my own home.

We returned to the States, and I remember the final hug at the front door and my words to my mother were, "try not to worry too much, and remember I am only a phone call away", and to my father I offered the words, "You have to fight this!" Again confusion reigned, my concern was sincere and part of me felt torn re my plans; I wanted to stay and continue to support and bring comfort. I also knew that I needed to return to our own family of three, and I knew that I could still help with supportive calls across the

Atlantic. Off we went to the airport, and the plane that would take me back to my beloved, and my child back to his own father.

Chapter Fifty

There followed months of phone calls and uncertainty, and a total feeling of being too far away. I used my life here mostly as a distraction, and I couldn't fully be in either country. Jonathan was, thankfully, settled into his school routine and we were fully occupied at the store getting ready for the busy season. I ordered whatever was needed for the store and kept everything meticulously up to date, expecting the phone call to, "come now" almost every day. It was a stressful way to live, and I remember, many times, saying sorry to my husband for not really being fully here. It was a crazy time.

They were given the date for the surgery, and a lot of things had to be put in place to make it as smooth an experience as possible. My mother wanted to be close to the hospital, and they had been told he would be there at least ten/twelve weeks. My siblings went to Dublin in search of a conveniently located apartment and found one in Sandymount, minutes from the hospital. It was comfortable for my mother and would accommodate any and as many of her children that were available to keep her company. They rented it for three months, and got my mother settled there the same day that my father was admitted for his pre op. It was the best decision ever, as this apartment gave my mother a home from home base where she could come and go as she pleased, and enjoy a little down time, in comfort, when she was away from the hospital. It also allowed all the family a chance to be there for her, and none of us would worry about where to find accommodation, in a busy city like Dublin.

The night before the surgery, I remember calling my father on his cell phone, all his visitors, even my mother, had left; it was midnight Irish time and 7pm for me. I had called the nurse's station first to ask if he was awake, and they told me he was, and that it was fine to call him. He sounded ok, worried about losing his power of speech and very afraid of his ability to cope with being knocked out, as he called it. He had tried praying and told me that the Bishop had called to wish him well and how much this meant to him. I told him that all his time spent in the Church was useless, if he couldn't summon up his faith to let the Lord take it from here. I reminded him that he was a stubborn old fighter and so not a quitter; I couldn't believe I was talking to him like this, but I needed to distract him from his pessimism. This was an unusual situation. He started to get sleepy, I reassured him that we would all be there to take care of my mother, and that he should focus his energy on getting better. Before I hung up, he asked me if I would call him the next morning; in a few hours, actually, before he went for the surgery. He didn't want to be alone for the short time before my mother arrived. I found this fascinating, but having been in a position of relying on a phone conversation myself, I agreed. This conversation with him also forcibly reminded me of his frailty and vulnerability. I began to see him in a totally different light. He was no longer able to be a control freak; the very situation necessitated reliance on others and I could see this was a terrible struggle for him.

I called the next morning and spoke with him for a few minutes, until he told me that my mother and siblings had arrived, and that he was ok now. I cried that morning for the uncertainty of it all and again I felt useless and far away. I really wanted to be there, making it easier somehow for my mother, and also bringing comfort to my father. I remember sending an email to Jennifer's dad and his wife, saying how hard it was etc....and the email I got back, "we're here for you", made it possible to be ok to be here. All of us, in this country, were on the phone to each other all that day and it helped. Later that night, my mother called and said the doctors were very pleased with how it all went, and that my father was in the ICU and resting. He would remain there for a few days and would continue to be cared for with round the clock nursing, until they had a clearer idea of how he was. We were all relieved that it was done, and ready for the next phase of updates and the all important answer to the question, "did they get all the cancer out?"

All of October, we got calls to keep us informed, and I chatted with my mother almost every day. My father's prognosis was excellent, the hard road right now was to recover and get adjusted to the fact that he had only one vocal chord, and that he would have to relearn how to swallow; food and drink. He was not the best patient anyway, what male is? But he was totally frustrated those first weeks, with not being able to speak. They had explained to him that this was temporary and that it would slowly return. He was not a patient person, and would lose his cool and throw the pad they had given him to write on, clear across the room. It was hard for my mother to see his frustration.

He was recovering well otherwise, and soon was up and about, walking around the hospital corridors.

We did reach a point though, when, after discussions with each other, one of us was voted to give him a pep talk. My mother was under enormous stress with the whole situation, and his expectation of her spending every waking hour there, was too much. He had nurses but she didn't. So he agreed, or was finally convinced, that she should relax at the apartment and after lunch would come see him, and stay till after the evening meal. This worked much better. Whichever of the twelve of us was staying at the apartment, would drive her to the hospital, see her safely in, and then, after a brief hello to my father, would go off and do their own thing. We would return to accompany her to the cafeteria for mid afternoon tea, and some fresh conversation. We all enjoyed the chance to chat and give her a break from the medical scene, and sometimes take her out for a brief shopping trip. She would return to stay with my father until 8ish, when he would reluctantly say goodbye to her, until the next day. Sometimes I wonder how she did it. And sometimes I wonder how a grown man could be such a baby! And need his children to set boundaries to aid his recovery! And safeguard the health of his wife, their mother!

I flew to Ireland with Jonathan mid November; I needed to be there, and planned a ten day visit. This would be our second trip to Ireland this year. We landed in Dublin this time and drove directly to St. Vincent's hospital. I was totally overwhelmed by all the changes; the city was completely unfamiliar to me. There were so many one way streets that I kept getting lost. I found the traffic intimidating. I wanted to turn around and go back to the States. I tried to get around St. Stephen's green and follow Merrion out to Dublin 4, but it had all changed and I was frustrated. I stopped and asked lots of people for directions, and I finally found my way and parked the car.

I felt unsettled, and quickly asked myself again what I was doing here. I had forgotten until this moment that the last time I had been here, was as a patient dealing with my own serious issues. It hit me with a wallop to my heart and my head! I went to the bathroom and stood against a wall and took deep breaths, and talked myself into being calm. I prayed myself along the walk through the hospital. We followed the signs up to the Unit, and I walked the corridor looking for the correct room. I stopped and looked in, and I saw an old man sitting half asleep in a chair beside the bed, and I thought, "This can't be my father, this guy looks too old". I continued to walk to compose myself and when I was ready I turned back, went in, and he opened his eyes. I am sure he thought he was hallucinating when he saw me, and he immediately started to cry, but he was delighted. We chatted and at least by this time, much to my relief, he could talk, if only in a whisper.

He was thrilled to see Jonathan, and thanked him for all the letters he had sent, saying they helped him get through his bad days. I said how well he looked and tried to conceal the shock that I really felt. I said how long we would stay and he was delighted at the chance to see us so often, and he said it was great the way we all pulled together to work it out so well. Did I know that my mother had not spent a single night alone? I hadn't known, but it didn't surprise me.

We all felt a strong connection to my mother, and probably would all share the sentiment about experiences in our childhood, when we felt him to be the one in the way. Many of us felt that he blocked her in some way, from being the mother we wanted and needed, and that's the main reason, I think, why she continues to have so much of our support. In due course, that day, I found my way to the apartment, and my brother jumped up and down, literally, when he saw me. "Jesus, where did you come from?" My mother couldn't believe it and was excited at the change of pace, now that we would stay with her for a while. We returned with her after lunch to the hospital and spent some time chatting and catching up. At 4pm, we escorted her for afternoon tea and she was visibly relieved to sit and enjoy a scone, and tell me how she herself was coping.

She agreed with me that he was a terrible patient, and I was thrilled to give her an opportunity to vent. Life's a bitch, Mother, try it out, you will feel better, just having said it, and I can still hear her laugh and telling me how awful I am. Jonathan loved that cafeteria, with all the mini individual sized packets of Irish cookies and cakes. We stopped at the little shop, and bought a paper and some candy bars and returned to the patient. This would be the routine for our time there. It was such a comfort to be there with my mother; a chance to spoil her and take care of her and ease her burden in any way possible. I found myself less worried also about my father; being with him in person was much more reassuring, than any phone update could be.

In the evenings, we would return to the apartment, and enjoy a meal together, Jonathan and I. After some homework and some TV, we would drive back up to the hospital, and my mother would be ready to leave and return to the apartment, to enjoy being home and done with going out for another day. I will remember those evenings always; driving in the dark to the hospital, it was November and winter time, pulling up to the A&E entrance, watching

Jonathan eagerly head up in the elevator and a couple of minutes later emerge, with my mother by his side. He used to jokingly offer her his, "granny arm", as he helped her from the hospital door to the car. He was only ten years old, and I marvel at the emotional generosity he displayed to us all, and his understanding of the difficulties that we were all coping with.

One day, as a treat, she agreed to go out for a meal, but I could sense her guilt because he wasn't with us. Another day he was being especially cranky and so I took her off shopping for a couple of hours, and gave him instructions to, 'raise the level' and not be such a crank, or we wouldn't come back at all. It was like talking to a child in some ways, I had so much empathy for him but it annoyed me when he made my mother feel bad, especially as she had been doing so much for him. I may have been more emotionally generous toward him, but my tolerance for even a glimpse of his old ways was zero.

As it had been years since my last visit to Dublin, myself and Jonathan took a bus into town one day and walked all over and explored. We went to Trinity College and got to see the graduates pose for pictures, a fluke that it's graduation day. Such a fabulous college and just peeping in you have a mental image of academics wandering the hallowed halls. Then we went on to O'Connell Street, which, years ago, was a hive of activity, and now was almost empty. We wandered into Easons and indulged in Annuals; Judy, Bunty and Dandy, reminders of Christmas past! Jonathan spotted a Kylemore that looked delicious, and so we had tea and our signature cream buns! It was fun, and we rode the bus back to the hospital full of stories of all we had seen. My father listened to my son recount his adventures, and Jonathan remembered the warning from Nana not to tell Grandad about the cakes; as he loves them too, and you know he can't swallow yet. We sat at the side of the hospital bed and looked through the Annuals, and some of the stories are the same ones from forty years ago, and it gets me going. Talking about memories and Christmas morning and how we would all swap with each other, and how glorious it was, and my father interjects with, "So we did something right, some of the time anyway". I could hit him, but the guy has a hole in his throat! So we let it go.

While we were in Dublin, one of the Harry Potter movies was released, and that was another afternoon that Jonathan and I took for ourselves. He loved the novelty of a movie theatre so far from the U.S., and afterwards we took our time walking through the Dundrum shopping centre, where the multiplex was located. He called his Dad from the car and filled him in on what a great afternoon he had, and all about the movie. I was glad to give him this afternoon for himself and a chance to feel, in a small way, that we were on a vacation of sorts. When we got back to the hospital, my brother and his wife and son were visiting, and it was great to see them again. We all went back to the apartment and Jonathan got to spend time playing with his cousin, while the adults compared noted on how we thought things were going for both of them, the patient and my mother.

One morning, I drove around the village of Sandymount, an odd experience as I had lived there in the 80s. I was so not that girl any more, and I had no sense of anything except being so far from that experience, and if I felt sad it was more a reflective feeling; it was such a pity that I had to go through all that to get here! I wandered down the main shopping area and found a hair salon, where I would insist my mother should go and indulge in a relaxing time for herself. I set up an appointment for her and looked forward to dropping her off next morning. I continued to drive around and went toward Ballsbridge and turned on to Simmonscourt Road as if on autopilot, and came to a stop outside the Poor Clare Convent. I used to come here when I lived in Dublin, the grotto in the courtyard reminds me of the Ursuline, and my sister and I used to go to the grille and chat with the nuns. They were on retreat now, it being Advent, so I left a note and continued on, glad that I had had the chance to stop by. The next day we had more family up from Tipperary, and again it was a blessing to get a little taste of what we had given up, by having to stay in Dublin. I was so thrilled that they all made the effort to come up to the city, and it made the hospital time easier, not just for me, but for my mother too. These visits also cheered up my father and the ensuing conversations deflected attention from the tension of the medical prognosis, and allowed him to engage in everyday life.

It is time to leave again, and it's not so hard; I know he is in recovery and I am reassured that my mother is coping. I will leave and one of my siblings will come and keep her company, and she will get through this, and be home for Christmas. I leave happy because I am going home too. On the plane home, Jonathan shares with me that he didn't feel like he was in Ireland at all. We didn't get to Tipperary or the beach, or any of our usual haunts. I agreed with him that because of all the time in the hospital, this was a different kind of trip. We promised each other that next time we would go back to our usual Ireland, and we felt better just talking about it.

Chapter Fifty-One

Our Holiday season in the States was extra welcome that year. Having been to Ireland twice, the break from work and routine was more than welcome, as we were seriously in need of some time, just for us. As usual, after my time in Ireland, I went through some deeply thoughtful times and I had an epiphany of sorts yet again; as some more of my issues with my father were resolved. I had thought that I would die before him; remembering my time at that hospital as a patient myself and thinking how fragile I was. Here he was, at this time, a mortal being after all, and no more in control of the universe than anyone else. It was reassuring to me to see the separateness from him yet again, and how the power of all his many words from that past life could no longer reduce me. I embraced this feeling and told myself that it had been a long time coming.

We welcomed the New Year, 2006, with our wish for good health for all and a release from the stress of illness related travel, especially to Ireland. The first couple of months went very smoothly, with the store taking up the bulk of our time, and we welcomed the routine of everyday life with no surprises. In March, my husband's cousin celebrated his 50th birthday, and his wife planned a surprise party. He was the eldest cousin and as per Armenian tradition, viewed as the patriarch of this generation. As my husband really loved and admired him he planned to go. It would be eight hundred miles round trip, so he and Jonathan would take a few days off and go together. I happily waved them off and looked forward to some time to myself.

Jonathan brought his video camera and would show me everything when he got back. They had a wonderful weekend. The party was at an Armenian/Turkish restaurant, not far from New York City and it was a night of good food and dancing. They were all thrilled, not only that my husband attended, but that he had brought his son. It was also a fabulous chance for him to catch up with the cousins who had flown in from Istanbul. I spent the weekend indulging in reading and not cooking a single meal, and chatting with my sister; she was en route to California from Virginia.

Jonathan turned 11 later that month and as a surprise we gave him the ultimate gift for a Lego addict; a trip to Lego Land in California. He screamed when he opened the gift and saw the airline tickets. He was such a Lego enthusiast; we had given him a room just for his Lego at the house. He had built an entire town, complete with trains and an airport and even an entire section devoted to Harry Potter and another to Carousels. Everyone who saw it was stunned and recently when he chose to pack it all up, as we got it ready for storage, he was nostalgic about all the hours of fun that it had given him.

We left Virginia and flew to San Diego and on arrival we took a taxi to Carlsbad and the resort hotel that was minutes from Lego land. I will never forget the look on his face when, the next morning, we stood in front of the gates and everything was made of Lego. There are giant Lego people all over the roof and along the side walk. Inside we viewed the mini cities, exact replicas of New York and San Francisco, all made out of Lego. The most fun for Jonathan was the chance to get a driver's license and drive a Jeep made from Lego, he had to do this as often as our time there allowed. We took a boat ride to see the 'around the world' Lego attractions; the Taj Mahal, the Eiffel Tower and the leaning Tower Of Pisa. It was the most incredible experience and worth the trip just to see the awe and sense of recognition that Jonathan had everywhere he went. Before we left we found some difficult to find pieces for his collection and had them shipped. We spent some time also on the beach; it was a different experience to be by the Pacific.

My sister had been driving to California from Virginia and it turned out she would arrive while we were there. She made our hotel her destination and it was so fun to stand in the lobby and welcome them out of the car after their cross country adventure. She had always felt that she would end up in California and I always knew that at some point she would make the move. We sat on the roof top deck of the hotel that night, looking out at the city lights glowing and the Pacific close by, and wondered at the odds of our being there at the same time. It was an anxious time for her as she had no definite job or home lined up, but who was I to tell her anything, except go for it, because I had been in the same place not too long ago. She was euphoric with courage and a dream and I knew that given six months and some luck she would make this town her home. And she did.

I always think that of all my mother's eight daughters she was the one that got the roughest deal. She is one of the second set of children, and with a strong personality and an inclination towards adventure proved a challenge to my father. Her spirit was cracked in many places but thank God never broken, and each time she overcomes an obstacle I stand in awe. She is the one, despite the challenges she faces personally, that will be delivering hot stew to the neighborhood when there's a storm, a hurricane or a power outage; I have seen her do it. She is the one who watched my baby while I comforted Jennifer's dad, she is the one who took care of Jennifer when I had my surgery, she is the one who had Fintan move in with her when he had no place else to go, she is the one who went home to take care of my mother when she had surgery, and she is the first person I want to call when there is any news from home. I think sometimes that she makes choices that make her life more difficult, but I have to remember that she is the one living it, and in the end, it's her life and her choices to make. I enjoyed our shared time in California and it was easier going back to Virginia knowing that she was no longer wandering the highways; she had arrived. Even though we had had a marvelous trip and Jonathan had memories from Lego land that would last a lifetime, it was bitter sweet to leave, as I was leaving my sister behind.

The news from Ireland continued to be good, my father continued to improve and with time his voice got stronger. He had been to the Hospital for a week long treatment of isolation radiation. He was confined with no visitors but was fine with it as he felt it was a better way for him than chemo. My mother was in better form now that the treatment seemed to be working and she knew he was getting better. She was of course also thrilled to be back in her own home. She enjoyed the visitors to the house and started to go on shopping trips and short excursions. She would go and have lunch with her brother and sometimes her sister, and I am sure this was all helping her to re charge, as it were, before she returned to take care of my father and be a support for him. They were seeing life with renewed appreciation, having gone through such personal trauma.

We welcomed the summer weather and the end of the school year. After a week at home when school finished, we headed off to North Carolina to enjoy the beach. It was such utter bliss to be able to ride our bikes and enjoy the peace and quiet of the small village. We would walk on the beach first thing in the morning, standing looking at the ocean and just taking a minute to be still. We ate when we liked, mostly whatever we picked up at the farmers' market, and we slept whenever we felt like it. Jonathan and I sat beside each other by the pool engrossed in our books and I remember looking over at him and thinking, let him always have the comfort and joy of words.

After dinner we headed back toward the mainland to browse the stores and just enjoy the freedom from routine and the schedule of school and work. If it rained we went to the movies. This is my American version of the beach of my childhood. I could stay there forever; the minute I land I am at peace with the world and the smell of the ocean and the sand under my feet is, I feel, as good as it gets. It's a feeling all three of us share, and whenever we want to get away the beach is always the first choice.

In August we returned home to attend an event that was months in planning. The Irish Tenor was coming to sing at a local Auditorium and our store had been one of the sponsors that made it possible. One of our customers at the store was chairman of the committee planning it, and knowing that I was Irish, came to invite us to be a part of the event. I thought this was pure karma. We sat in the Auditorium tapping our feet to the music and being transported to the Emerald Isle. It was a fabulous concert with all the old favorites like Danny Boy, Molly Malone, The Hills of Athenry and many others. We got to meet the tenor when it was over and he was thrilled to have someone from home in the audience, and Jonathan was the proud recipient of his autograph.

Later that month, my cousin and her husband and their two children were coming for a visit. She lives in Ireland during the school year and in the States during school vacation. She is the epitome of the frequent flyer. She chose to do it this way; not willing to choose between the two countries and loving the life she has in each. She wanted her children to experience the Irish education that both she and her husband had experienced themselves, and so this is how she set it up. She is someone you want to be around, she probably kissed the Blarney Stone more than once because she never stops talking. It's a good thing because she is observant and intuitive and great at sharing. Her children are a joy to be around, they and my son just go off and play and they entertain themselves. He never has to worry that they will demolish his Lego room, as he knows from previous visits that they always ask for permission before they touch his display, and have an appreciation of the work he puts into building it. She always brings a supply of goodies from home, and we always end up laughing and joking in a way that I never would with my American friends; mostly because we speak the same language, no explanations necessary. We jump all over the place with topics, which is such an Irish trait, and nobody else would be able to follow. She lost her father after I lost my brother and we both talked at both of these times, and I think the grief and loss and the isolation of being away from home gave us a common bond for this friendship to start.

Sometimes I think I live vicariously through her; chatting with her after her time in Ireland is almost as good as a visit there myself. When she visits we spend time at our store, as the extravagance of the setting and the designs always amaze her. We always hit the department stores also and I allow the dormant shopaholic in me some time out when she is around. At the house we talk for hours, covering so many subjects its mind boggling. My husband, as he passes through the nearby kitchen with fresh tea or coffee, en route to resume his game of pool with her husband, has the impression that we are speaking in Irish! We don't see each other that much but as each holiday approaches I know she is on her way back to the States, and I get ready for my lengthy phone conversations and my fix from home.

As usual, the end of the year brings the time to focus on the store and all the prep work that goes into everything being in place when the busy season rolls around. After nine years of doing it we have it down to a fine art. We each have specific jobs to do and work side by side, knowing the path each of us is on will meet up, when we are ready. I love this time of year. The weather is beginning to cool in a more predictable pattern and every year the joy of the first sweater does not lessen. For me the biggest trial, living so far south, will always be the climate; I have gotten used to the long months of heat with temps always close to 90 or 100 degrees and above, but I will never get to a place of enjoying it. Each year I am sure to say many times that whoever invented AC was the #1 genius of all time.

This year, to celebrate our 15th Wedding Anniversary, we decide, because we are so ready and organized at the store, to take a break and spend a few days at the beach. North Carolina in October is pure heaven, we walk onto the beach and as usual the ocean air is like a drug and I surely inhale. My husband and I walk hand in hand reminiscing as one does on anniversaries! , and it's pure simple pleasure to walk in the sand together and watch Jonathan in the distance try to get the wind to take hold of his kite. We sit and look at the water and talk about the countries in the distance. We marvel again and again at the life and luck that brought us to this place in time. We stay the weekend and return home refreshed after this little escape to our own world and our favorite place, and we all three feel the blessings of nature stay with us.

Chapter Fifty-Two

The news from Ireland is that yet again my father has successfully gone through another week of the Isolation radiation. My mother, meanwhile, enjoys the time to herself to recover her own balance, with the comfort of knowing that my father is well taken care of at the hospital. The holiday season is approaching again, and I remember, after a phone conversation with her, I had a strong visual of her enjoying the comfort of her own home. She had had a particularly good day, as a friend of my brother's had brought her a fresh Christmas tree and set it up in the bay window of her living room. She said the whole house smelled of Christmas and she mentioned that it was so delicious to have a real tree. The fragrance compensated for the needles that might drop on the carpet. She had the fire lighting as there was a chill in the air and her sister had come with her husband for afternoon tea. I could feel the contentment in the sound of her voice as she spoke; I saw the three of them drinking their tea and warming themselves by the fire, admiring the tree and each dreaming about the holiday to come and the reunions that would take place.

After they left, she sat by the fire with her book,

comfortable and, for once, no one to think of, except herself. Taking a well earned rest and talking on the phone with her children when they called, and taking the time to say thanks for a lovely chat. I always remember her calls ended with " it was great you called and thanks for giving me all that time, it was a lovely chat" , and off she would go and read again, until the next person called. At these times, I didn't feel far away, I felt glad of my own life and almost as if we were both having the same experience, except in different places. She brought me comfort in her own comfort and I could go off myself and read a book and feel the connection between us.

Our own holiday season that year went as usual with family coming in from around the country. My sister in California called and shared via the phone because it was too far for her to travel and be with us in person. I had shipped a Christmas cake to her, and we had the usual screams of delight on the phone. The store continued very busy and we were seeing the time just fly by. We talked with everyone in Ireland on the day, and we still marveled together that it had been over a year since my father's surgery, and how thankful we all were that they could celebrate the season in their own home.

We rang in the New Year, 2007, watching the local fireworks display. It was cold and it seemed right to want to rush home and enjoy a fire. We were happy with our own lives; being together and enjoying the store, and we gave thanks that Jonathan continued happy in school and was proving he could more than handle, even welcome, the academic challenges. My wish for that year was that things could stay on an even keel; that we could have some continued time without the stress of wondering if a trip to

Ireland might be imminent. My wish was granted, I think, as the year moved forward we settled into our own lives and were able to enjoy home life for ourselves and mark our own family days for each other, without any distractions.

In March, Jonathan turned twelve, and we wanted to surprise him with something special. He had developed a serious interest in Robots and computer programming during his previous semester at school. He won the Science fair with a robot he had programmed to identify color and follow directions. This was an interest he developed and pursued in his own time, so I knew it was important to him. I knew the perfect place to take him was Cape Canaveral and the Kennedy Space center. We put the tickets and the itinerary in a big box, and when he opened the gift on the morning of his birthday, he was literally speechless. "Are you kidding me", he asked over and over, and began to cross off the days on his calendar as he waited for departure day to arrive. I was so excited myself that I couldn't wait to go, thinking, if he is this thrilled just at the idea of it, imagine how he will be when he is actually there.

We headed down to Florida during the Easter break, and when the plane landed in Orlando I could hear Jonathan's heart rate speed up! The taxi brought us past the Space center and he looked out the window imagining what discoveries lay behind those walls. We checked into the hotel and after dinner on the patio, surrounded by palm trees, we walked out to explore and enjoy the Florida scene. For the next few days we soaked up NASA and my child devoured it! He stood in awe in the history museum as we followed the trail of discovery. We could sit in the shuttle and take a moment to imagine the astronauts before departure, and be in awe of the power of intelligence and the search to understand.

We had lunch with an astronaut, sitting opposite English and German tourists, and Jonathan had a new found appreciation for his American heritage. This was the American dream at its best; the appreciation of something and where it might lead. We continued to view, again and again, so much history and Science blended together, and it was no surprise to me that Jonathan had no interest in exploring any other part of Florida during this visit. He wanted to spend as much time as he could in this one place and take home as much as he could possibly remember. The highlight, for both of us, was taking part in a reenactment of a shuttle lift off. We went through all the steps and listened to a list of precautions and preparations, and then heard the final countdown and the horrific, ear splitting noise, as the rocket shot into the sky. We all stood with our mouths open and our eyes filled with wonder, and it wasn't even the real thing! Again, this is a memory that stays for a life time, the appreciation of the history and what we can learn from it. My son became aware that there is a great deal to be learned from those who paved the way.

Over the summer that followed, we had our usual time in North Carolina and as always felt renewed and refreshed after our time there. Conversations with Ireland were peppered with my parents thinking about the idea of a trip here. In the beginning, I didn't take them too seriously, but as they continued to bring it up, I thought it might happen. I remember talking with my other siblings here; my sister in California and my sister in DC, and one brother in another part of Virginia. There were only the four of us here now; the others having returned to Ireland in search of whatever it was they needed. All would settle back in Ireland eventually, except three, and it's still amazing to me that each did whatever they needed, and followed their instincts and ended up in exactly the right place for them.

It was with not too much surprise then, that I heard flights had been booked, and the parents would visit all of us later that year. Their intention was to start in DC, go from there to California, and then come to us for the last leg of their travel. Needless to say, many phone calls took place once their plan had been announced. My sister in California, especially, was anxious. She had not had too much interaction with them since leaving Ireland, and was feeling a rising sense of possible judgment and coming up short before the parents had even left home. I consoled her and reminded her of the possibilities and a chance to let them see her as her own person. At the very least, remind herself that their visit was a moment in time and that she could continue her independent life after they left. We were all crazy and its hilarious now to think of all this back and forth stuff that went on, but I think it's just how we are. We all reassure each other as we know the score, and we know what it takes to have your protective gear on, because you never know when you might need it.

And so their trip began and the calls among us continued. We were like a behind the scenes security detail, "they are here from the airport, chat, eat, all OK, talk tomorrow". It was nuts, but we felt better because of it. It was as if, between us, we could keep track of them, and there was no room for surprises. For me personally, it was not an anxious time; I felt secure enough in my own life with my husband and son, my business and my home, that I honestly felt that they were just visitors to my life. When it was time for them to come to us, my sister in DC drove to a convenient location on the Virginia side of the city, and we all met for lunch. It was fun and they were both delighted to see Jonathan and catch up on all the news. My sister had enjoyed her time with them. I think we were all aware of the fact that these two people were mere mortals just like the rest of us. We were also finally acknowledging that they would not always be around and some of our own intentions were clearer; we wanted a better relationship with them, they were our parents after all, part of who we were. It wasn't about forgiveness for past behaviors; it was more an acceptance of ourselves and a pride in going beyond, more despite, than because of. It was almost 4pm when we left the restaurant and I was anxious to get as close as possible to home before dark, so we waved goodbye to my sister, and she knew that she would see them again for their final night, before their return to Ireland.

We arrived in Virginia and my husband was waiting with a welcome and an offer to help with their luggage. It was a great evening that followed; they were happy to be cozy in a home where it was obvious that the three of us loved and cared for each other and were happy to share. They unpacked their suitcases and Jonathan was the proud recipient of his favorite Irish candy. I was glad to see my Odlums' flour and the ground almonds vital for my marzipan for the Christmas cake. My husband got slabs of the cross cultural Turkish delight. They had brought all the other Irish necessities also; the tea bags, Bisto, brown bread mix etc. We spent two days relaxing and enjoyed showing them the store and loving their awareness of all the changes and improvements since their last visit. My father, observant as always, missed nothing. He spent hours just looking at everything. My mother enjoyed the jewelry and while she leaned on one of the showcases for support, I noticed a new fragility about her. It was a scary observation and I felt sorrow that she too was changing and that her health was not as good as I had hoped. On their third day we packed up the car and headed off to North Carolina, echoes of Kerry and our home beach never stronger. I was almost tempted to bless myself and start the rosary! But that wasn't my style.

We enjoyed the drive down, glorious countryside side by side with the highway, my father enjoying the mix of makes and models of cars and talking to Jonathan about how many different types there were. My son was thrilled to be on vacation; out of school while all his friends were not. About a week before my parents' arrival, I had emailed all his teachers explaining that he would take a week off. I asked for no homework assignments and said that they would no doubt agree with me that this was an opportunity he needed to be free to enjoy. I wanted this child, whose view of his grandparents I had very consciously not obscured by my own experiences, to have a chance to have fun and show off on his own territory.

We arrived that day and ate lunch looking out at the ocean, and my mother said she could see why I loved it there. We walked the beach before we went to the house and all four of us marveled at the beautiful weather in late October. Our days there were spent on beach walks and kite flying, on home cooked dinners and sitting around the table playing scrabble. My mother and I took time for ourselves and shopped, again with the approaching holiday season in mind. I saw again that she was easily tired and stopped sooner than I might have, for some rest. I took care to make the excuse of a cup of tea so she could sit down.

It was an oasis of time; I felt the past slip away, as the idea of my child and my father playing with a kite or a Frisbee was no longer something in my mind, but before my eyes. I felt the joy of my own bravery and the acceptance of the effort it took to be here, and I thanked God for the chances we get over and over, to allow the life we are intended to have, to emerge. I knew my parents had enjoyed this time also and that they too could see how I had built a bridge to join the best parts of the old and the new.

We had a couple of quiet days at my home before their travel continued and we spent those days mostly listening. My father was on a roll one night, talking about his mother and remembering his own childhood and youth, and I wanted to soak it all up like a sponge. I couldn't hear enough and I only wish now that I had asked some more questions, but at least I got a pretty good view of the life he himself had lived, and he confirmed my previous impression that he idolized his mother. My mother also talked about her family; her sisters and brothers and life at the farm. Jonathan was fascinated and was a perfect audience. I was delighted that we all had this opportunity; to truly get a glimpse of the real lives of each other.

They left soon after, and would enjoy one further night in DC, and fly to Dublin the next day. I think they both returned home tired, almost exhausted, but they must have had a sense of some resolution. If nothing else, they got to see the next generation and how change continues to unfold. For myself, I knew this was a trip that I would be happy to remember, as I strongly suspected that this would be their last time undertaking such a strenuous journey.

My mother's frailty was hard to see and I didn't want to be reminded of her new limitations, but I knew she found it more than usually difficult to be away from the comfort of her own home, and the easy demands of the life they had established for themselves. I gave thanks, yet again, for the gift of the time we shared, as I knew my own resolution and peace increased with each visit.

Another Christmas arrived and this year it was just us; we had had so much family here while my parents had been around that we were sorely in need of time just for us. The three of us settled in to enjoy each other that year. We still observed the traditions, but took time to appreciate our own small family and to give thanks for the blessings that continued to come our way. We talked to everyone by phone and felt connected to the Irish gathering in a new way; the parents so recently having visited.

Chapter Fifty-Three

We rang in the New Year, 2008, and once again happy to see what it held in store for us. We talked with all the family in Ireland and my husband's family in New Jersey and echoes of 'Happy New Year' were heard around the States and across the Atlantic. Jonathan returned to school, happy and content and loving the challenges and doing well academically. We continued to enjoy the store and couldn't believe this was our seventh year. We, in an effort to get more involved in the community, had joined the Chamber Of Commerce, and also National Jewelers associations. We chose local charities to support, and expanded the awareness of the store by having a more extensive advertising campaign, through various sources within the community. Work continued and my husband was always expanding the designs and we were building our reputation of being exclusive and creative. I was busy with tax preparation, as was usual for the first two months of the year, and I liked to get our paperwork done early. Life was busy and productive and we loved every minute.

Jonathan was now 12, and would turn 13 in a few months. I began to think about his Confirmation, as this is the age to be confirmed in Ireland. I made an appointment to see the pastor of our local Catholic Church to discuss it; the usual age for the U.S. was 15/16. I explained my thoughts and how I would like him to follow the Irish/family tradition and we had a lengthy interesting discussion. I explained to him that I had gotten the text book for the sacrament from Ireland and that Jonathan had already been studying, and also that he took Scripture/Bible as an academic subject at school. He appreciated the fact that I had such strong feelings and understood the ties to my Irish traditions. He wanted to meet Jonathan and then he would take it from there.

We set up the appointment, and after chatting with my son he told me he was charmed. He loved the fact that Jonathan was so open about his personal faith and especially how he defended the Godliness of his school environment, and here the priest said to me, "as of course it's not Catholic"! I found this comment hugely entertaining, but I decided not to get into it! The pastor submitted a letter to the Bishop in Richmond and we waited to be told that this child was deemed ready for Confirmation. It duly came, and Jonathan was delighted, as indeed was his Mother! We continued to do the prep work and he had one final discussion and then he was done; he would be confirmed in May.

At the end of March, he celebrated his 13th birthday; we marveled at having a teen. He wanted a celebration with his friends to mark the event, and so I chauffeured the teenagers to a movie, followed by pizza and games at the house. It was consoling to see them still into laughing and joking with each other, while shooting sponge pellets from guns and rifles, and flying remote control helicopters into the trees behind the house. It was a fun evening and we savored the chance to see a happy carefree 13 year old with so much joy for life, and so much anticipation of where his life might take him. He was well on his way and our only prayer that night was that the Lord would guide us through these teen years which we knew would be nothing if not interesting; and that has proved to be the ultimate understatement! He was a great kid, but even we knew that hormones and the search for independence were coming, and as his parents, we felt the need to acknowledge it, and be glad we had each other for reassurance.

The excitement started to build again as the day of the Confirmation drew near. My father and older sister were arriving for the event. Jonathan was thrilled that his beloved Godmother could be his sponsor and he was delighted that she could come all the way from Ireland. My brother would also be here and my sister was coming from D.C. Jennifer's dad and his wife were also coming, as no celebration at this point would be complete without their presence. We took Jonathan out to get his Confirmation suit, echoes of the Irish writer Frank O'Connor for me! And he chose a fabulous dark formal with a silver shirt and red tie. He was inviting some friends from school, and staff members were also aware of the upcoming event. I was happy to see the connection between school and home and church.

My preparation was mostly in the kitchen, as I baked our Christmas cake recipe for his special cake; it would be the centerpiece for the celebration that would follow the event. The Confirmation was set for Friday evening, and on the previous Wednesday, we drove to the DC airport to pick up the arriving Irish, and we talked our way back to Virginia. It meant so much to me that they were here. We were sad that my mother couldn't make it but the flight and travel would have been too much for her. My sister had brought the traditional white name tag with a red confirmation ribbon, from our old school at home; they had recently had confirmation there and Jonathan's card was included as a special gift. I remember saying to myself, "could it get any better than this?"

My sister and I spent the day before putting together our usual feast and were so happy to be doing it. My mother called and we filled her in and double checked with her about a recipe. Jonathan and my father went off on their usual rambles around the neighborhood, with my father enjoying the trees and the lake and the sense of being in the country. When Jonathan was at school, my father would head out with Sasha on her leash, and find the trails through the trees and take turns until he found his way back. Sometimes he took a nap and I realized that the travel had taken its toll, and I remembered his health issues, and encouraged a slower pace.

The big day arrived, and Jonathan appeared in all his finery with the white and red name tag in place. It was like seeing the past come alive; we remembered our own confirmations, all twelve of the family and I am sure my father found his mind wandering back also. We got to the church and the foyer was packed as crowds gathered to greet each other before going on in. I spotted Jennifer's dad and they came over and I remember thinking, once I caught sight of the others in our group, we are all here now. Jennifer's dad came over to chat with Jonathan and straighten his tie. They stood on the edge of the group and I snapped a picture, and in my mind I saw Jennifer smile. The ceremony itself was beautiful with the traditional hymns "Come follow me" and "Ave Maria". We proudly watched as Jonathan and my sister stood before the Bishop, and Jonathan bore witness to his faith. We stayed after the ceremony to meet the Bishop and take pictures, and our pastor took the time to tell my father how much trouble I had gone to, to make this Confirmation happen, and he ended by jokingly telling him, "this is all your fault, you started it". It was apt, in so many ways.

Later, we returned to the house and Jonathan and his friends did teenage justice to the feast. We joked and we teased in the time honored Irish tradition. The pace of the chatting sped up as it always does and the volume increased with enthusiasm. Jonathan opened his gifts and cut his cake and we enjoyed every minute and every bite. I can still see my sister, en route to the deck, telling Jennifer's dad how handsome and charming he was and that he was only getting more so with age, and he told his wife, "you see; that's what I'm talking about, and why I love to come here". All this delicious banter was one of the reasons we loved to get together. I savored every word and wanted to hold on to the memories forever.

We had another five days with our Irish guests and it was a time of sitting around talking and just enjoying each other's company. One night, my sister and I headed off into town by ourselves and left my child, his father, and grandfather, to play pool. Another evening, we all sat around drinking tea and indulging in the Irish goodies they had brought and listened as my father talked and told stories of his own years growing up. When do we get a chance to do this? I remember thinking that I only wished I had it all on tape, because I am sure we didn't remember every word. It was a different experience with my father, because this was the first time for me to have him visit without my mother. He seemed more relaxed, only because I remembered that last time she had seemed more frail and we were all, not just he, conscious of watching out for her. I also realized that he was still dealing with the cancer and struggling with side effects. When home in Ireland, he continued to go to the Dublin Hospital for periodic checkups and treatments. The few days, just being around the house, were restful and he looked good when the day came to do the return flight to Ireland. We drove to DC and it was hard yet again to say the goodbyes, but I again gave thanks that they had been able to be a part of such an important stepping stone in my son's life, and I was especially thankful that my father, despite his failing health, had travelled so far to join us.

Only weeks after their departure, the official start of the summer arrived. School was out and the ocean/beach was calling. All three of us loaded up the car and headed south, and had our usual collapse by the ocean and were happy to be there. We biked all around the place and took different routes and trails to see where they might lead. We sat on the beach late into the evening while my husband fished. On the really hot days we cooled off by the pool, read our books and took a nap. We got up early to watch the sun rise and walked together on the deserted beach. We gathered shells to bring home and sent the flat stones that we found skimming back into the ocean. We went to our favorite restaurant, glad that it was so early in the season, and so had no wait. We sat outside, overlooking the pier and indulged in seafood and long cool drinks. We saw the reflection of ourselves and captured it as the definition of summer. We returned home tan and healthy and full of the joys of the free and easy days.

The next month brought a first for Jonathan; we had agreed for him to fly to New Jersey and spend a week with his Armenian grandma. All the family was thrilled and delighted, as they had invited him many times and couldn't believe that he was finally arriving. We waved him off at the airport and he happily boarded, playing the experienced traveler despite this being his first solo trip. He had no idea how nervous his mother would be until the call arrived to say he was safely there. He had an amazing week and it was a great experience for him to be with his Armenian side of the family for a change. He went to a Turkish restaurant in New York and recounted to his father every morsel he consumed. He went to St. Patrick's Cathedral and strolled down 5th Avenue. He went to family barbecues and was amazed at all the cousins coming together in one place.

He got to spend time with his grandma and see her prepare her specialty dishes, just for him. He made us jealous and wished we lived closer. He got to play with his younger cousins and feel superior; he is the eldest child of his generation. He came home full of Yaya and family, and a closer connection to his father. He also had a new appreciation of where we had started and how we might have stayed up north too. I was glad he had this opportunity; I knew that as he got older, strong family connections would matter, and he needed to nurture these relationships.

The end of summer came as quickly as the beginning and the only unsettling news was from Ireland. My father called to say that my mother was starting to be unsure and uncertain, and it was causing him to worry. She might set the table for three instead of two, and talk about there being too many people in the other room, where there was no one, except perhaps a TV on. He was going to make a Doctor's appointment and would let us all know how it went. Within the hour, we were all talking to each other, and everyone in Ireland promising to keep us up to date.

It was a worry for me also. She seemed ok most times when I called, but I had begun to notice some odd references during phone calls, and I had put it down to tiredness. My father, meanwhile, was doing fine with his own health; he had started to put on a little weight and was looking as good as he had in years. There were seven siblings at home at this time, four very close by and the other three within a few hours' drive. I decided not to be overly concerned until we had a better idea of what we were dealing with. I was also in contact with both my mother's brother and sister and they shared their concern, promising to keep in touch with me and give me updates after their own visits with her. It was the end of October by this time, and I was glad of the distraction of work and the store; I knew that keeping busy over the next couple of months would leave me little time to think.

The holiday season passed, with a family Thanksgiving with guests, and then we celebrated Christmas with just us. My sisters were celebrating in California and their goodies and traditional foods had been mailed. We were very busy at the store leading up to the holiday season and my husband and I agreed that a quiet Christmas was what we needed. The one memorable event that season, as 2008 came to a close, was the election of the new President, Barack Obama. I remember being on the phone with my sister in Cork, Ireland, on Election night. It was the middle of the night for her but she was as excited as me. The excitement we felt was indescribable as we watched American history be made as he was announced the victor. We both listened as he gave his speech, full of hope and optimism; a shot of faith in the future and the good things to come. We even talked about the difficulty of the job he was undertaking and how so many of the problems would take years to solve. The sense of intention conveyed in his speech was not something America alone needed to hear, but the world. I remember, as we hung up, both of us were feeling the impact of his words and already we were planning on connecting again, on Inauguration day, in January 2009.

The New Year arrived, and on January 20th, Inauguration day, we, the nation, and the world, took part in the celebration. I allowed Jonathan to take the day off from school to enjoy the ceremonies on TV and be part of the crowd watching history be made. It didn't matter what your personal politics were; it was a day of change for America and we were all eager to be a part of it. I remember calling my sister who had shared the election night with me and we both listened together to the new President's words to the world. I called my Dr./ friend in Dublin and joked about my new allegiance and sense of belonging. He reminded me how hard I had worked to get to this place and I enjoyed the sharing and sense of accomplishment. We also scared each other, more than a little, by talking about how long we had known each other, and how many years I was living in the U.S. It was a day for counting blessings and making connections with the living. I talked also to Jennifer's dad and we agreed that this was a positive day for the country, as we savored the moment and didn't dwell too much on the monumental task this guy, our new President, had taken on.

That winter, we certainly got a taste of Mother Nature being fickle; it was the coldest Virginia had experienced in a long time. We got the snow shovels out and enjoyed the novelty. Jonathan loved his snow days, and especially loved that his mother called a halt to life as the first snowflakes began to fall! I loved the feeling of snuggling in against the elements and relying on each other to stay warm and fed! We always prayed that the power would stay on; power outages causing the greatest hardship in bad weather. For the most part that winter we were lucky.

The news from Ireland continued mixed; my mother had had a fall over the Christmas celebration and was unsteady at times since. I had noticed a subtle change when I talked with her on the phone; sometimes her comments were out of place. I let it go though, not wanting to deal with whatever it might mean. In February, my sister in DC decided to take a trip home and see how things really were. She called and told me the change in the mother was frightening, that she was forgetting things and getting mixed up re where she was etc. However, at this time, she was still strong enough to continue, perhaps at a slower rate, the preparation of meals and other stuff related to keeping the household running; thus allowing all of us to deny that the problem was serious. My father was due for another checkup back at the Dublin hospital, and my sister stayed with my mother for the duration. There was no question of her being alone, as the chance of another fall was too great.

Meanwhile, life here was busy; for me tax season was around the corner, and again I was of the mindset to keep everything up to date in case I needed to leave, and was preparing the returns early. I knew from talking with home, that the central issue was now becoming our parents' reluctance to acknowledge that they were not going to be able to continue by themselves for much longer. In April, my mother was admitted to a Cork hospital by a referring cardiologist and she had a surgical procedure to take care of a blockage in an artery in her neck. She was weepy and sad and uncomfortable when I talked with her on the phone, but making sense and well able to chat about how she was feeling. I was relieved. My father travelled on the train to see her and she felt lost when he would leave. It was a strange time for all of us; difficult to understand their relationship and how connected they were, and trying to balance that with our own memories.

We couldn't help but wonder at who this weeping dependent woman was, who only a few years ago had supported her husband for twelve weeks post surgery; away from her own home and in a city that may as well have been another planet. It was so hard to clearly define any of it and the best we could do was let her know that we were there to support her. She was released from the hospital and returned home to recover. Perhaps they both wondered at this time what changes they would be forced to make in the coming months.

During the last months of 2008 and the early months of 2009, with frequent phone calls from my husband's family up north, we knew that my young brother-in-law, Alex, was battling serious health issues and having a hard time. We all shared many phone conversations and kept up to date with the various Doctor's appointments. My husband got a call, in early May, from one of his older cousins to say that it might be a good idea to come and visit, that Alex would benefit from some added encouragement. My husband spent a day getting the store ready to function without him and headed up to NJ to spend a few days with his family. He went alone, as my son and I both felt that this was a time for him to be with his mother and his brothers. Alex was admitted to the hospital and I remember the phone conversation that night with my husband. I listened as he tried to find some understanding and a way to offer support, to his mother and brothers, while he was there. They all felt, and had also been told by the doctors, that the situation was very serious. Alex was in serious liver failure and while he was on the transplant list, the prognosis was not good. My husband said how fragile and sick he had looked and he was afraid for him and for all of them.

Apart from the reconnection with family and the difficulty of his brother's health situation, my husband was dealing with all the changes since he had last lived in New Jersey; almost fifteen years had passed. I remember he talked about the noise level, and the traffic jams and the struggle everywhere to find parking. The contrast between the new setting of our lives and the slower pace of life in Virginia hit him on the head like a brick. He returned from that visit with a renewed sense of appreciation for his family awaiting him, and a sense of helplessness and grief about his brother. I identified with him on so many levels, having experienced similar feelings on returning from Ireland. We talked a lot that week about his family and their own particular demands and restrictions and we allowed for Alex having had his own struggles. We commented on how inept in the end each of us is when faced with insurmountable struggles.

He went again the following weekend and again for the longer Memorial weekend, each time driving toward the hospital and trying to stay positive. They had great conversations, he and his kid brother; reconnecting with each other and Alex so appreciative of their chance to spend time together. He kept saying how proud he was of Jonathan and how smart his nephew was. His message to me was that he would come for a long visit as soon as he was better. He joked with his family about missing food cooked on the barbecue and begged his cousin to bring some in. Each time my husband returned I saw the conflict written on his face; the sense of wanting to be in both places at the same time and the resentment at neither feeling right. Again, it was an echo of a place I had been myself.

Back in our own lives in Virginia, Jonathan was all set to graduate from Middle school and there was a special awards ceremony and dinner to mark the event. All three of us went to school that night and enjoyed the celebration of achievement and the marking of the next stage, as Jonathan would move to the school's High School in September. It was a lovely evening of being together and seeing Jonathan all dressed up, and the girls complimenting him and all the classmates joking together as they got ready as a group to move on. When we returned home that night, the red light flashing on the answering machine led to a conversation that informed us that Alex had been placed on Life Support. He would survive only another two weeks; it was a terrible shock and I remember thinking we must have been in total denial because we had truly expected that at the end something would save him. There is something surreal about someone so young dying.

After receiving the terrible news, there followed for us a couple of very busy days as we cleared the orders and repairs due at the store. My husband had engagement rings and wedding rings and anniversary gifts to be picked up. Our customers were used to personal attention from the Master Jeweler, and he needed to contact everyone and assure them that all was ready and that the staff would take care of them. He worked for hours to get it all done. Meanwhile, Jonathan and myself were packing and making sure we had everything for the trip north and for the funeral services. We left Virginia early, and almost eight hours of driving later, we pulled into a hotel parking lot, about twenty minutes from the family home. We opted for the hotel because no one really had room for three people, and also because I wanted myself and Jonathan to be able to leave and have our own space, while my husband had some alone time with his family. There was no question of seeing Alex and this was hard, so we went to his mother's house and joined the crowd gathered to mourn.

It was tough for me; the first death since my brother and I was feeling very mixed up and extraordinarily vulnerable. We met all the cousins, aunts and uncles, and we all shared the sense of shock and outrage. We all had happy memories of Alex and we tried to get through it by sharing and just being together. There was a huge buffet and we all ate; reluctant to leave and reluctant to stay. We finally got back to the hotel around midnight and thought of nothing; too drained after the hours of travel and the gathered grief, we surrendered to eight hours of well needed sleep.

The following morning the funeral was set for 10 am. We had arranged to go to the family home for breakfast and so we did. I observed the same shaking of the head that I had seen with my own mother. Pain and confusion was the norm; it all seemed so familiar and I felt so helpless. There was something surreal, as I think there always is at a time like this, about continuing to do ordinary, everyday things; how could we be sitting here drinking tea and eating toast when we would never see Alex again? We all tried to just get through it. When we arrived at the church we saw that the coffin had been placed at the entrance. We all followed behind, as a procession, into the church. The service was a mixture of English and Armenian and full of scripture quotes and lamenting. I felt a strange lack of comfort and

I craved the familiarity of my own traditions. I wanted a celebration of life and a reminder and acknowledgement of who Alex had been. It felt cold to me after my experience of the personalized Mass in my own church, and there was no one with whom to share these sentiments. It took self control not to feel judgmental and shocked when my mother-in-law screamed and roared and banged the lid of the coffin, questioning and screaming why this had happened. Her outburst left me feeling even worse; so much empathy for another's pain and no outward way to express it. I missed my own family and how we physically comfort each other and felt alienated by this stand alone sort of grief. I don't for a minute doubt that it was genuine; culturally this is how it is done, the volume of noise in direct proportion to the void felt. But for me it was too much. It served to allow a feeling of disconnection with my own husband, and I wondered at having taken him away from his family and his own way. Intellectually, this was nonsense, but I couldn't free myself from these negative thoughts that continued all the way to the cemetery. The burial was also neutral, with no reference to the son, brother, nephew, cousin no longer here, and again I felt the being apart and not belonging there.

We proceeded to the restaurant after the service and after the meal my husband went with his family to a gathering at his mother's house. They all continued to find comfort in each other and to share their memories and their grief. It had been a sad day, and for me, extremely difficult; not having someone from my own family there, or a close friend, to allow me to view the whole proceedings in a detached way. I felt it all so personally. Anything I said to my husband would feel like a criticism and instead I had chosen to say nothing. We returned to the hotel and Jonathan and I rested and strolled in the surrounding garden area.

Later that evening, as Jonathan and I ate dinner in the hotel dining room, we were surprised to see my husband appear at our table as we hadn't expected him so early. He said he had told his relatives, "I have to go back and spend time with my own family now". This brought me enormous peace; his way of saying the three of us together were his family, and I remember thinking this trip is not all of who any of us is, it is just a tiny little window into his life as it was. I needed to go home, and so the next morning we were up very early and hitting the highway and halfway home just as the sun was coming up. We both appreciated the long car ride as it gave us time to discuss our feelings about the events of the past few days; it served to reconnect us and I felt my own balance return.

Once we arrived home, we relaxed and my husband continued over the next weeks, to speak of his family and his loss. From our conversations, I knew that, for him, there was no sense of having given up or lost out. I still felt uncertain myself and profoundly sad; layers of loss spilling over each other and I knew that I needed some help to resolve my confusion. I spent a couple of days chatting with my Dr/friend in Dublin, until I was able to understand more fully what had happened. I was able to give myself some credit and acknowledge the natural sense of alienation when surrounded with the customs of a culture different to my own. It was another time when my Divine Providence came to the fore yet again; I continue to value the voice at the other end of a phone line and give thanks for the gift it continues to give. And I also reflect on the ongoing consequences of the earlier disconnection for that young girl that continues into adulthood.

Chapter Fifty-Four

During the weeks after we returned from the funeral in New Jersey, I spoke a few times on the phone with my mother. I knew for sure that something was seriously wrong; she was detached from what I was saying and giving inappropriate answers and comments. I was devastated and felt the immediate sense of loss even though she was still here. There was another appointment set up with the cardiologist and we would get an update after that. I had to be happy with this as I was so far away and there was nothing else I could do.

Jonathan was on summer vacation and enjoying his time off with friends and working at our own store to earn some extra money. He was also committed to a course at William and Mary, the local University, on creating a short animation movie and he was really looking forward to it. I kept busy with work myself and tried to be patient as we waited for news. My sister from DC arrived to celebrate the July 4th holiday and we welcomed the distraction and being able to talk about home. We were all in the same boat; separated by distance. We did a barbecue and sat outside and later played board games, and watched a movie. A couple of days later my mother was called for pre surgery screening so we knew a definite date was on the way.

My brother arrived for a visit at the beginning of August, en route to Ireland; he was moving back, this would leave only three of us here now. My mother was having her surgery on the 12th and he wanted to be there and be able to stay for longer than just a visit. Jonathan and I had planned a trip to New Jersey for mid August and we decided to stay with the plan and go. We drove up enjoying the sights along the way, and easily found our hotel close to the Jersey Shore. We were planning to take a drive around the State! We planned to visit the locations where my husband and I used to live, and I would show him his parents' old haunts from before he was born. We had so much fun! I showed him the old Victorian house where we had lived with the large front porch that had been the site of so many parties. We drove past the church where we had been married and the school where I used to teach. We drove by Jennifer's home at 91 and saw the imprint of time passing; her dad and his wife had moved so it was a stranger's now. We travelled up Bloomfield Avenue and marveled at the changes; so many stores had moved location and so many new roads and houses had been added to the landscape. We saw that the same restaurants were still there and we even stopped at the grocery store where we used to shop every week. From there we got on to the Garden State Parkway and headed north to Westwood and Ridgewood, and drove around and saw the school where we held the Irish club and the language classes. I hadn't been there in fifteen years but I still found my way, landmarks suddenly familiar helping me along my way. We found the import store for all things Irish but not so well stocked as in earlier years; the owner telling us that the internet was now his competition. We indulged for old time's sake!

That evening we asked directions to the train station and decided to go into New York. It was called Little Silver, all quaint buildings and cobble stones and seemed unreal for such a short distance to the city. Once again, I got lost! and marveled at the locals having to deal with the volume of traffic on a daily basis. We travelled in to Penn Station and took a taxi up to the Rockefeller Centre. We had my husband in Virginia on the cell phone; vicariously visiting these streets with us and touring New York too. We went to St. Patrick's Cathedral, wandered along the city streets taking in all the sights as we went and enjoyed the novelty of eating food from a street vendor. We fought our way through the crowds and wondered at the contrast to the peace we loved at home. It was surreal in many ways and delicious in others. We got on the train and headed back to our hotel, excited, as tomorrow we would spend the day with Jennifer's dad and his wife.

We enjoyed seeing them in their new location; they had moved to the Jersey Shore. It's so different and yet not, they have managed to bring the charm and welcome with them to this new house. As always, I think of Jennifer, and know she would get a kick out of my baby coming to spend time with her Dad! We had some delightful chat and delicious food, and browsed through pictures and reminisced, and caught up on all the news. I am seriously impressed with all the fabulous landscape design; beautiful lush gardens and stone walls and pathways. We are all the same really, carving out a niche for ourselves to create an environment with our own particular stamp. Later that night, we returned to the hotel to rest, before hitting the highway early the next day for the long drive back to Virginia.

The update from Ireland was that my mother's surgery was over and that she was recovering. She would be transferred to a Nursing Home to recover. She was very agitated even at the hospital and my siblings had to take turns to stay with her as she was not happy to be alone. On August 19th she is moved and I talk to her on the phone the next day, and all she does is cry. I can't imagine how upsetting it has been for her; first the hospital, then the surgery and now, not able to be in her own house. No wonder she was bewildered. I am sure she was wondering if she would ever go home again.

I started to think about a trip to Ireland, but knew that the window of opportunity was small. Jonathan was due to start High School and I didn't want him to miss out on any of the startup experiences. I talked to her again the next day and she was joking around; about my brother when he came to visit and how she wanted him to cut his beard, and had asked the nurse for a scissors! It was so good to hear her sounding like herself and I hung up feeling better. However, just a couple of hours later, I got a call from Ireland to say my mother had had a heart attack and had been taken by ambulance to the Hospital. My heart sank, and then I said, "Enough of this indecision, just book the flight and go!" ----and I did.

I was flying out on the last Sunday in August and early that morning the phone rang, and thinking it was from Ireland, I answered; it was sad news for my husband as we heard that his friend Richard had died just hours earlier. We were stunned, and I couldn't help thinking, "dear Jesus, could we catch a break, enough already!" My husband went over to the house while I finished getting ready for our flight. It was a crazy feeling; wanting to go and wanting to stay. I felt sad to leave my husband, and was only reassured when he reminded me that he would spend all his time away from the store, at Richard's house, with Richard's wife and family. I felt this was the best thing for him.

We flew into Dublin and drove down the country. I had no cell as my American one didn't work in Ireland! I looked everywhere for a public phone box but no luck. I later learned that Ireland is the mobile/cell phone capital of the world! And so no public phones. I ended up stopping at a hotel in Abbeyleix, and called my family from there to see how my mother was doing. She was still in the hospital and there would be no update until later in the day. I remember thinking, "thank you Jesus, keep her safe".

My uncle and his wife had booked a B&B for me in Cashel, as I preferred to be independent, and when we arrived to check in they had left an Irish mobile for me, Praise the Lord! I was thrilled! Communication! Jonathan and I took a nap for a couple of hours and later headed over to the hospital in Clonmel. My parents were both there together when we walked in. My mother was frail but very much herself and all chat about our flight and how great it was to see Jonathan. We had an hour to ourselves with them before the rest of the gang descended and we got to meet everyone almost all at once. I was delighted to be home and relaxed into the joy of the anticipated time with my mother over the next week.

That night, my mother was moved to a larger hospital in Cork, and so I decided to go ahead and rent a house close to my home town, and base ourselves there; the B&B was great for one night but Jonathan and myself were used to creating a home from home base for ourselves and we would be more comfortable in a house. All the family would come up and down and it seemed the best plan. That way, if the family got to be too crazy, we had our own space to escape to. We spent the next day at the hospital, meeting with my mother's sister and sensing her anxiety about the whole situation. My mother was able to talk and enjoy our company, and it was reassuring to actually be able to see her. We brought her food from outside and she enjoyed it. My brother got a wheelchair and brought her down to the chapel and the gift shop, joking with her as they went, so she didn't feel bad at being unable to walk that far. She enjoyed all the interaction.

It was only when it was time for us to go that she got upset. I remember coming up the stairs one evening and seeing her crying as she sat in a chair outside her room. She was such a desolate figure and she sounded so upset. There was a nurse trying to comfort her, and she agreed with the nurse that she had been through a terrible time and was entitled to cry. I put my arms around her to comfort her, but she started complaining about being left alone at night and how she hated it. So from that night on, my sisters took turns to stay with her, and once she knew that was the deal, she calmed down and there were no more tears.

Cousins and other relatives all came to see her and it was fun bumping into them all. Jonathan and myself took our usual time to ourselves and went around Cork one afternoon, and explored and shopped for the trip home. I saw few friends this trip as we were so focused on the hospital. My father was returning home every night, so we spent a couple of hours there some evenings; Jonathan had his computer and showed my father some games, and these were a great distraction. Another evening, I dropped into the convent, my old Alma Mater, and chatted with the nuns and was shown my mother's name at the top of the prayer list in the chapel.

Jonathan was at the public library, which he loved, as there was guaranteed internet. Any time I needed to see someone and I knew he'd be tired of the constant chat, I would drop him there for a computer session.

On my second to last day, I drove to Cork by myself, leaving Jonathan with his Godmother. There was discussion going on re my mother only being allowed home if they would agree to set up some home care and help. The doctors had explained that there would be no more surgeries, this was it, and she could be at home and see how she did. She would be close to her children and they could come and visit.

Imagine getting these two to agree to home help! Their own interpretation was that we were asking them to agree to the house being invaded by strangers. I tried not to laugh but really it was too ridiculous. I remember sitting with my mother and telling her that she deserved the help; hadn't she worked and taken care of everything all these years. I reminded her of my father's domestic limitations! He was barely able to boil a kettle! She smiled at this and nodded. She needed to hear that the house was still hers and that she would need to tell whoever was helping what needed to be done; this in an effort to allow her to believe that she still had some say in the running of the household. I explained to her that this was the only way she could continue living at home. She agreed and I could see her mentally calculating it all and gradually coming round to the idea. I also said how lovely it would be to sit by the window in the sitting room, with a fire going and a book to read, and there to chat to whomever showed up. I made it all sound so appealing, I almost wanted to stay and enjoy it myself! I was comforting myself too with all this persuasion; I wanted to return to the States knowing she was feeling positive about the next stage of her life and that she could be happy.

My father really was useless around the house; he was capable of vacuuming a carpet or filling a dishwasher, but God! He wanted it always acknowledged and he'd almost expect an award. It was too trying. But having worked on her, I knew he was next. He was coming on the train so I went and picked him up and gave him an earful all the way to the hospital. I could see he wanted her home and he too was coming to the realization that they couldn't manage alone. This was all I could do. The next day I hugged my mother goodbye and told her to eat well and rest, and then before she knew it she'd be home. She thanked me for coming and for all the chats and off I went. We stayed that night with my father and I had to eat my words, at least mentally; the next morning, he had breakfast ready for myself and Jonathan before we left for the airport!! Well now! I was pleasantly surprised and couldn't wait to tell my mother, and everyone else!

We flew into Dulles and my husband and my sister (then living in DC) were waiting for us. It was such a joyous reunion. My sister was delighted to be able to see us and we gave her all the updates and all her Irish goodies, and after a quick cup of tea in the cafeteria we headed south for Virginia. As usual, after a trip to Ireland, I couldn't stop talking; I wanted to share every second of the time there. I also, as usual, couldn't wait to get back to my own house. My husband was delighted to see us; it had been a hard week as he had spent most of it with his friend's wife, helping her sort everything. There would be no burial, instead, a cremation, and a memorial service at Arlington in about a month.

Richard had served in Vietnam and was a Purple Heart

recipient. It was a sad time for all three of us as we all loved him. He used to come dressed as Santa for Jonathan and leave crazy gifts for us on the front porch. Having heard that I loved nutcrackers, he left two full sized ones outside the door one Christmas Eve. He and my husband used to go away, every six weeks or so, for a guy weekend. They would drive to State parks or another city and just enjoy a meal and chat. Both being Armenian they had a great deal in common and Richard was a solid life presence for my husband. He was our go to guy for advice; always bouncing ideas off him before we made any definite plans. He was such a big part of our lives and now we had to try and continue without him. He used to call the store every day, sometimes twice, and on a weekly basis stop by and bring lunch, and so even day to day stuff was hard. He and his wife were always there for family events and all of the landmarks in our lives. It would be a difficult transition but we tried to help each other through it.

Jonathan returned to school, the start of High School, and he settled in very quickly and was happy with all his classes. Like all parents we watched him that morning and thought how did this happen? Where did all the years go? We were busy at the store; both of us trying to make up for the time away. Life continued, and my mother came home from the hospital on September 8th, their 54th Wedding Anniversary. The family was delighted and as I spoke with them that evening they all sounded optimistic.

In early October, we drove to Arlington for Richard's memorial service; it was a beautiful ceremony with full Military honors. We watched the gun salute and the ceremonial folding of the U.S. Flag and felt honored on Richard's behalf and glad we could be there. There were speeches from the guys who had served in Vietnam with him, and we all got goose bumps to hear such detail of a life lived before we knew him. Later, there was a reception at the Officer's Club and again we got to share stories with everyone there, and I know my husband, especially, found comfort in this opportunity to pay tribute to his beloved friend.

Toward the end of October, we celebrated our own Wedding Anniversary. There were lots of calls from Ireland and around the States. Not unusual for me, I had a great chat with Jennifer's Dad that morning. They had been such a central part of the wedding celebration that my mind always went back to New Jersey and Jennifer and the location of the festivities. Probably motivated by all the loss of the past year, I wanted him to know how much I appreciated all that he had done for me. His response, guaranteed to bring a smile to my face, then, and always, "right back at you kid!"

November and December passed uneventfully, we continued well at the store, busy and working long hours. Jonathan was finishing up his 1st semester of High School and had happily adjusted to all the changes. My parents were doing ok, my mother still chatted when I called and sometimes, sitting down to her afternoon tea, she would say what a pity I couldn't just drop in for a cup. My father was having a hard time adjusting to her continuing forgetfulness and wandering around the house. We had to remind him many times that none of this was intentional, that she needed understanding and empathy, instead of his frustration. My siblings were coming by to help out more each day and supplement the in home care. My mother's brother and sister also visited and I was glad sometimes of the more objective updates from them. That Thanksgiving and Christmas it was just us again; it was a hard time of missing friends, especially Richard, and we just wanted to stay home and enjoy time away from the store.

The New Year, 2010, arrived with a bang; freezing temperatures and possibilities of snow! The State of Virginia hadn't seen a winter like this in a long time. Schools closed and everyone was out with their shovels clearing the driveways and sidewalks. We were thrilled and loved being home together and in survivor mode in anticipation of a power outage. We cooked pots of stew and soups and watched movies snuggled up together against the chill outside. It was peaceful and calm and I remember thinking that sometimes Mother Nature gives us just what we need.

At the end of January, my mother was back in the hospital; this time for a two week stay that would help monitor her condition and promised to predict a better and more accurate prognosis. My sisters would call and tell me how awful it was to see her back in the hospital, so helpless and sad, but we tried to console ourselves knowing that she was well cared for, and that my father was also getting a break. I continued to stay in close contact and allowed life here to keep me busy.

We had another memorable blizzard in early February and the chill continued through the month. Jonathan returned to school, and my husband and I enjoyed more time together as we slowed the pace of going to the store in the morning. It was nice to start the day with a leisurely breakfast. We had both noticed that we get tied up with all that is going on and sometimes forget to take time for ourselves, and the store was in good hands with our staff. In March, it's another St. Patrick's Day and we chat with family and friends around the U.S. and also in Ireland. We have friends over for dinner and I restrain myself from making the mashed potatoes green! Jonathan is decorated for the day; a reminder and a smile for Jennifer. On my mother's birthday, at the end of March, she celebrates in style and she is thrilled with herself. My father gave her flowers and her favorite perfume and lotions, her brother brought her a beautiful rose bowl of blooms from his own garden, and cup cakes that his wife had made. She had her birthday cake made by one of my sisters and all her children came by with cards and gifts. Her phone never stopped ringing and when I talked to her later that night before she went to bed, she told me it was her best birthday ever!

Just days after my mother's celebration, our son turned 15! It was a quiet celebration, being mid week, and he was busy all night editing a movie that he was working on for school. That weekend he did the usual movie and pizza with friends. It was a relief to us that they could all get tech free and take a break from texting also! We were enjoying this stress free time of regular life and it was such a joy to not have any distractions. Easter rolled around, and my cousin was back from Ireland for the holiday, and so we chatted and she filled me in on all the news from Ireland. Toward the end of April, I started to think of the summer, and allowed my brain free rein visualizing being in Ireland once again. I thought of the luxury of time with my mother and a chance to see for myself how my father was doing.

The news from Jennifer's dad and his wife is that they also have been thinking of a trip to Ireland, and I don't need any prompting, I email them immediately with suggestions, and let them know how thrilled all of the clan at home will be to see them. They set off mid May and I am all but on the plane with them! I know their itinerary, so follow them in my head and see them as they travel through Dublin, to Dun Laoghaire and across the country to the West. They visit Achill Island and marvel at the untouched scenes before them, but I think they find it too raw. They make their way down the West coast via Galway, where they are saddened by the evidence of Ireland's economic struggle; they drive past many streets with boarded up store fronts and empty houses.

They continue down the country, and arrive in Tipperary, and they call me when they pull up in the central square of my home town. Oh, isn't life grand! I get such a kick out of their being there, all the more delicious as I suffer no envy; my own trip in the works for August. They head out to Two mile Borris and the quaint village welcomes them, it is a peaceful resting place, after all the travel. They are impressed with the new motorways but saddened at the automatic bypassing of all those beautiful villages. They visit my family; dine in my sister's for lunch and visit my father for an afternoon, sad that my mother has just days before been transferred to a Nursing Home. They see all the childhood pictures on the walls and see the portrait of all 12! They go to the Horse and Jockey and laugh and are entertained by two of my brothers and my sister. They are overwhelmed by the welcome, and feel part of the family as surely as if they were. As of course for me, they are! They enjoy every minute, and all this enthusiasm gets me going myself, and I am thankful of having booked my own trip and can now look forward and enjoy.

Jonathan, meanwhile, gets a very prestigious invitation; to join an International Student Conference being held at Harvard University at the end of June. This invite is in recognition of his excellent academic record. We are thrilled for him and so proud. Everyone at school is proud also and he ends the school year with lots of good wishes and reminders to be a good representative for his school. We relax for the two weeks before he has to leave, leisurely picking up what he needs and enjoying dinners on the deck, just the three of us. My husband and I can't quite figure out what we'll do while this only child of ours is away, but we rationalize that it's good training for his for real full time college departure, getting closer by the day.

We drop him at the airport when the day arrives and once the plane leaves we head off together. We feel like newlyweds, it's too funny. There is nobody around for whom we are responsible. We shop for ourselves and take our time strolling around and then find a restaurant and dinner for two. Our son calls while we are in the restaurant; he has arrived and is having barbecue in Harvard Yard and his roommate is from Burma, and he has to go! We enjoy the rest of our time and realized that we would have no problem getting used to it's being just us.

Jonathan called every night and each time we got a quick synopsis of his day. The history of the college appealed to him and he was especially thrilled by the fact that former President Kennedy had stayed in the actual dorm where he was sleeping. He also shared that President Obama had a desk for study in the Student lounge. He loved the whole experience and hoped as he returned home to receive more of such invitations, and he shared with us how he felt the possibilities for his own college choice had now broadened.

After Jonathan returned from his trip, and after my husband and I readjusted to our responsibilities, we settled in to enjoy a few weeks together before our trip to Ireland. Father and son went off to the store a couple of times together and enjoyed their days, both learning from each other. I enjoyed the chance to go shopping and pick up some gifts for home and to get a head start on packing. They all knew we were coming so there was great anticipation on both sides of the Atlantic. My husband's brother was coming to spend time with him and so I didn't have the usual concerns of his being alone and lonely. The time to leave arrived and I worried as we loaded the luggage into the car that I'd be stopped for my baggage being too heavy; we were well over the limit. Luckily when we checked in for the domestic flight, from Richmond to JFK, New York, it was checked through to Dublin and I heaved a sigh of relief that there was no issue.

The layover in New York was long; six hours. Jonathan couldn't see why we wouldn't take a taxi into the city, but being all the way out on Long Island and already a nervous traveler, there was no way I was leaving the airport. We entertained ourselves with laptops and movies and games, and at 6pm, boarded the plane that would take us home, again!

Chapter Fifty-Five

Arriving in Ireland I knew this was a different kind of visit and going to be very special. I savored the usual welcome via the pilot when the plane landed. Ireland's temperature at 5.30am was 52 degrees, the forecast called for dry, some sun, scattered showers and the usual mix of Ireland's unpredictable or predictable weather, whichever way you looked at it. We walked off the plane and I was feeling so excited to be there I almost forgot the luggage. Ours was first off and we grabbed it and headed out to arrivals. We were not renting a car this time; my sister was travelling in France and generously offered me her car, so we bypassed Hertz and walked outside to the beautiful crisp morning, and five minutes later saw my sister coming toward us from the parking lot.

She was excited, as we were, and we hugged and jumped and I kissed the ground! We headed out onto the motorway and proceeded to zoom along, commenting on every field and blade of grass we passed. We drove my sister nuts; the two Yanks! Admiring the scenery and the green and the rainbows, and breathing in the air as if oxygen deprived. I was truly happy to be finally there and it was just so great to be home and I wanted to miss nothing!

We arrived at her house in record time and ate her delicious Irish breakfast, my nervous stomach suddenly gone, now that my feet were firmly planted on Irish soil. We got updates on everyone and talked about who we wanted to see and where we wanted to go. We headed toward town and stopped at my parents' house, my father still in his PJs, and the kettle boiled and the brown bread cut and the rashers in the fridge if we wanted them. It was so great to see him looking so well and I gave thanks for the opportunity to come visit. I looked out past him at the rolling hills behind the house and the green grass that stretches forever and it's a mental snap! And then walked to the front door and looked across at the farmer's yard and the cows grazing and did the same thing. I remember remembering and I wanted these pictures firmly imprinted in my mind. I returned to the kitchen and Jonathan is busy recounting his summer so far and my father is listening to stories of Harvard and President Kennedy and students from all countries. His eyes are open wide and I see the pride on his face and the thought, "this is my grandson!" I nod my head absently, while mentally thinking, "Well, actually, he's MY son!" I feel myself pulling away and a separateness that seems fitting stays with me, as I leave. I suddenly see that he is no longer a threat or a power that's ready to change me; I am here as myself with no doubt about what that means and I find myself looking forward to coming back later.

Next on our travels, my sister's business, where the house we had been raised in was now almost unrecognizable. Again the kettle is on and there are scones and cakes from her bakery and we hug and laugh and stay a little time, talking and catching up with each other. I walk to the yard and take a look at the view that I saw every day growing up. Snap! The stable far back with the paddock now a garden with seats, and the empty field next door, where we always lost a ball; now newly built houses and busy. I stand a moment and see us all playing and enjoying the outdoors and see too, my mother at the kitchen window, calling someone to come in and help, dinner almost ready. I rejoin my sisters and we hug again and off we go in search of my mother.

We park and follow my sister as she leads us through the entrance hallway and through a room to where she sits. She turns and sees us and her face lights up and I think, it's ok, she is here and so am I, and now it's all fine. She kisses us all and is so excited and thrilled to see Jonathan; how tall, how grown up, how handsome! She wants to know where we have been already, remembering the always frantic visits of our first day; wanting to see everyone all at once. We tell her about the visit to my sister and give her the scone we brought for her morning tea, we don't mention my father for fear of upsetting her and she lets us lead the chat and nods her head. We kiss her again before we leave, with promises to come back in the afternoon.

We park in the middle of the square at the centre of town, and walk around and meet and greet as old friends stop and say, "oh you're home from America, great! And how's your mother doing?" There is more chat and off we go as there are lots more people to see and we are greedy to meet everyone. I smile as I walk away and think this is it; this is what I have missed. I get used to being told that I have a terrible American accent and remind everyone that I have lived there over twenty years now, and tell the story of how I'm always told about the Irish brogue in the States. It seems you can't win either side; the other always hears the other! We get back to my sister's and what a perfect start to the day and it's only 11am!!!!!

Later that day, I head into town by myself, and drive straight through town and out to the Nursing Home. I park the car and that's when I see her, my first glimpse of the 'Woman in the Window' and that's when our journey starts. I will see her over the next ten days and my other alter life is going on parallel. This, my special trip to Ireland, has these two parallel paths running and I manage to navigate both, and get all I came for. Each day, during the time when I am not with my mother, I am adding to my collection of mental snaps. All my friends and family come to me, as this is one visit where I am not driving around to the towns and homes that I am in search of. This is the trip when I have said that I am staying put and at home, in my home town, feel free to come and visit.

My sister comes from Cork and we spend our first visit together eating dinner at a new restaurant, and as we say grace we think of all the family changes and how we are all adapting. Snap! All of us now, and then, flash through my mind and it's like an automatic update and seeing both visions at the same time. After the dinner we turn into the returning immigrants and head to the local Tesco, to grab to our hearts desire all the goodies of home that we miss and simply have to bring back. My youngest sister calls the cell while we are shopping and enjoys teasing about the American accents and guesses about what's in the shopping cart! She will be up later in the week, and so we plan to meet at the nursing home and then go somewhere for dinner. My sister returns to Cork that night, and on another day she joins us at our house and she and Jonathan explore computer software that he has brought from the States, and he thrills her with his knowledge and generosity with sharing. She tells everyone later how he showed her how to do stuff and the kid is how old? I think of my son, now 15, and feel proud of the job I have done, and how his growing up experience is so different to mine. I think of my husband and the joy that we both feel and the care that we take with this child, always. He has a proud Mama! Later my sister drives us to Holy Cross Abbey and we tour the church and grounds, free of people and priests, and snap! A new memory replaces the old, and I mentally forgive, but continue to feel sorry for, the priest of my earlier visit. We light candles and savor the holy peacefulness of the monastery, and remind ourselves of the life here, before it got polluted. I feel serene as we leave and remember all my childhood memories, when we used to bike out here and have picnics.

Another sister takes the afternoon off work and we go and visit the Newbridge Centre, famous for silver crafting and the generations of Irish who worked there. There is even a wall of remembrance as you enter, and after we see the displays, we head on up to see the museum. A collection of movie artifacts is here, preserving the decades long gone, with Marilyn Monroe, Betty Davis, and others. I see a tribute to Princess Diana and behind her a display and written history of Jacqueline Kennedy, I stand in front of this and snap! It seems ironic to be in Ireland, and take a picture of the famous Irish American Catholic Presidential couple, and feel the line across the Atlantic drawing shorter. I am grateful for my experiences and again feel the courage it took to leave and settle on the other side. We return later to my sister's home, and while Jonathan is entertained with his cousins, we talk, sitting at a table in her yard, of the earlier years and the time when our lives were shared. I am reminded of her kindness and offers of help and another snap! As I tell her how I felt and my sense of being thankful to her, and I feel at peace that she and I can go on with only a passing glance to what went before. We both know this and we both enjoy the discovery. We are both proud of each other and the way we struggled to what now is.

A few days later, I am sitting in my uncle's house, only miles from my beloved grandparents' farm, and while Jonathan discusses recipes and how to make his favorite cake, I sit and chat with my uncle. I go back on the memory trail and I remember more than he does and he looks at me in awe and sees how it was. We talk about the farm and all the holidays and how my grandparents used to be, and we end up talking as if they were still here and it's so much fun for me. We ramble on and on and it's another snap! I see him as he was and I am thankful he is still here; a wife and three children and five grandchildren later! He laughs when I remind him of that dandy guy getting ready for a night out and the effort put into getting waves in his hair. We leave delighted, both Jonathan and I, he with his recipes, and me with my pictures, and I can slowly see the trip home this time had a plan all its' own.

I sit another day with my older sister and again it's just us, Jonathan is off doing email and chatting with his friends at home in the U.S. We are relaxed and enjoying the quiet of her house after another crazy day of seeing everyone and anyone. She talks about the day my brother died and I now get more than "Fintan is dead". I hadn't known that she was the one, accompanied by a priest, to go and ring the parents' doorbell, and have my mother answer the door and 'know'. And see my father come out, a few feet behind her, to see who's at the door, and for him to ask "is it Fintan". Snap!

This new picture brings me comfort, an acknowledgement from them on the day, a knowing and with that knowing a certain sense of "Mea Culpa, Mea Culpa, Mea Maxima Culpa!" The Latin lines from the beginning of Mass so familiar to my father from the days before it was all English. I cherish this picture, because it replaces the Why? and the shaking of the head and brings peace to me and my brother. I thank my sister for sharing and we look back and remember together; the hardship and sorrow of those days, the comfort we found in each other. We still feel the sorrow, but we both understand more fully now my brother's search for what they couldn't give and he couldn't give himself.

I returned to my Alma Mater, to my friend the nun who had encouraged and tried to help/guide me during my last years in school. I see her on every visit home, but this time Jonathan seems more grown up and our conversation tends to stay in the present. He hasn't always joined me on these visits but today he is here and we wander, the three of us, around the grounds and the tennis courts and the convent walks. The very site of my earlier despair, where I look and see myself so lost, and waiting to be rescued somehow. I see the shadows of the people who changed who I was and where I might have gone, and in a moment see it changed nothing, and Snap! I see Jonathan and suddenly know that I am where I was supposed to be, and the shadows lose their power and I look around and smile, because the garden really is beautiful. We take pictures in the sunshine and turn and walk toward the convent and the afternoon tea that's waiting.

My mother's sister gets out of her car and gives me a hug and tells me "wait", she has something for me in the car. She hands me a large brown envelope and when I open it my mother looks back at me from before I was even born. It is a collection of photographs of all of the family in their days at the farm. Snap! The final link of theirs and mine and I want to hold on and greedily keep them for myself, which I will. It is mine after all because I will treasure it and there is nothing that could mean more to me. Later, I show her a picture of my mother reading to me, taken earlier in the week, and she looks and sees the likeness and is surprised, as I was. These are the links I thought about, and now they are real. I will leave here knowing that I got more than I came for.

I meet up with my friend from school and again I feel the difference; we can both share in a new beginning of sorts, the past is just that, the past. I can't have been seeing all this and not see it here too. My memory is in the present again, I am married now with a child and that is my life. She can see me clearly as I am now. Snap! The other me that I was in the past is now long gone from her memories. I can see clearly enough myself, to see it now too. We enjoy the updates and share plans and hopes and dreams. We each look to the future and see how it will be and are delighted to see that we share it.

One afternoon, having spent a couple of hours with my mother, I pick Jonathan up from the library, and we both drive out to eat supper with my father. Walking to the door I feel acutely my mother's absence, and Jonathan comments that he too feels strange because she is not here. My father is delighted that we have come, and the results of his afternoon's preparation await us on the table. I am touched to see that he has remembered my favorite foods, and that he has also gone to the trouble of having Jonathan's favorite Irish treats on hand. We spend the next couple of hours chatting and he takes the time to tell me how proud he is of the life my husband and I have created. He comments on the great job we have done with this child, his favored grandson. I find myself feeling sad again as I reflect back over the years; he is capable of being such a charming, personable guy, and it would have been nice to have had the luxury of this side of his personality as we were growing up. We had glimpses of it, but suffered the lack of consistency. I don't dwell too much on this reflection though; I am greedy to store up these happy moments and allow them to become yet another gift that this trip had in store for me. I feel empathy for my father and that is the predominant emotion inspired by this visit. He is dealing with the challenge of his own mortality and also with the changes that life's circumstances have thrown his way. As always, I am optimistic and hopeful, and allow myself to wish for some peace and acceptance for him; in his life as it is now, for his own sake, if not ours. For myself I have moved on; I no longer feel the pain and conflict of the past struggle and can recognize the autonomy of my new life.

One day, Jonathan and I take a day to ourselves, and head off like tourists to explore County Clare and The Cliffs of Moher. It is freezing and windy and there is the constant threat of a shower. We walk around the new Visitor's center and pick up some souvenirs to bring home, and then climb the endless steps to the top and look out and behold. We are literally speechless, it is so beautiful. We both stand there and can't help feeling thrilled to be together and glad of taking the day for ourselves. There is a harpist and a fiddle player and the place is enticing us to walk some more. We venture down the tiny well worn pathways, grabbing on to each other for fear of falling, and every step shows another view that's breathtaking. We stop at a beach on the way to the next village; having taken pictures every few minutes, there is just too much to take in. It's like looking at a postcard and you turn and there's another one. I wonder who I am here, this mix of Ireland and America, my child beside me, he too full of the wonder of the place.

On the way back to Tipperary I dial my priest/friend Fr. Tom, and ask about his times for saying Mass. We have an 8 0' clock tonight, he tells me, join us and come up to the house afterwards for a meal. We do, and it's another small morsel of Irish life to savor and tuck away for myself. His small country church filled with families listening together to his sermon of the gift of life and how we live it and share it, and I think how appropriate and apt. We all light candles, and then Jonathan and I wait, as he chats with his parishioners about their week, and I stand back and admire him for his goodness, past and present. We enjoy catching up at the house and he teases Jonathan about America and teases me about Ireland! He tells me of the struggle that continues to keep people involved and how the church has changed over the years, but he continues firm in his vocation and confident of the faith he inspires, and the lives he tries in every way he can to make better. I leave glad to know him and giving thanks for the help he offered me; a place to stay when there was nowhere else to go, and a chair in his kitchen and a place to cry the week after my brother died. I am proud that Jonathan knows him and through him gets a tiny view of what my Irish faith looked like when I was growing up.

All too quickly, it's my last day, but I don't feel sad or reluctant; I feel ready and grateful. This was a bonus trip, not just because of my time with my mother, but the time with everyone. I am still marveling at all the family/friends I got to see, and feeling eager to return to the United States and enjoy the sense of completion that I know is still simmering. In an unconscious way all the pieces have come to me and I need to take time to fit them all together. I can't let go of the idea of my mother enjoying the books and words so much, as if her frail and uncertain mind has taken her back to a stronger and more certain time. The value of words, so great already for me, multiplies over and over, until I can't wait to find the right ones to bring what she has given me to life.

A few days after my return, I find myself in the throes of a sort of crisis, and the only peace comes from the writing. I can acknowledge and treasure the gift of life to words through me and feel comforted, both by the writing, and the freedom that the words are bringing. It is as if my mother has given me her blessing, to wander back and find her and myself and bring us both together through all that has happened, and allowing for the understanding along the way. We see together the broader view of what she and I earlier only glimpsed and she knows that I will help her find the peace. Is that what she was looking for? Did she know that I would find the thread and pick it up and let it lead me? She always knew that I was closest to her past, her own start, and perhaps this is why she has given me the honor of the search, and why she trusts me to bring some new light and a beginning, not an end, for both of us. As I return to my life here, the comfort of the words has brought its own peace and for me a new beginning. I no longer feel the pull of conflict, rather I feel a reconnection of sorts and a joining together of the Irish and American parts of my life. I have a new understanding of what brings forgiveness and the lighter feeling that follows. I did after all find what

I was looking for, and that applies to both sides of that ever present Atlantic Ocean.

The End